HARD EARNED WAGES

— Judy McClard

HARD EARNED WAGES
Women Fighting for Better Work

Jennifer Penney

For my mom
whose wages were always hard-earned
and who deserves better

CANADIAN CATALOGUING IN PUBLICATION DATA

Main entry under title:
Hard-earned wages

ISBN 0-88961-081-9

1. Women — Employment — Canada — Interviews.
I. Penney, Jennifer, 1946-

HD6099.H37   331.4'0971   C83-098541-7

Copyright © 1983 by Jennifer Penney

Edited by Katharine Vanderlinden
Cover Photograph by Judy McClard
Cover and book design by Liz Martin
Typeset by union labour at Dumont Press Graphix
Printed and bound in Canada

Published by the Women's Educational Press
16 Baldwin Street, Toronto, Ontario, Canada M5T 1L2

CONTENTS

ACKNOWLEDGEMENTS

I am especially grateful to Judy McClard. Her ongoing encouragement, affection, good humour and levelheaded advice sustained me through all the fits and starts that marked the progress of this book. The other staff members of Women's Press — Liz Martin, Lois Pike and Margie Wolfe — saw me patiently through alternating bouts of enthusiasm and despair. Nomi Wall first suggested the project.

Many valuable improvements were made by Kathy Vanderlinden, who painstakingly edited the manuscript. Kate Hamilton transcribed a number of interviews and helped me out with several difficult decisions.

Donald Cole often and cheerfully assumed my share of childcare as well as giving me emotional and financial support.

As the work went on, collective members of Women Healthsharing taught me that I didn't have to be there all the time for things to go well. They tolerated several leaves of absence and coped with many unfinished tasks. The Bioenergetics Women's Group helped me to hear women with different perceptions.

Friends and acquaintances all over Canada were generous with suggestions, spent time arranging interviews, put me up and fed me during my travels. In particular, I want to thank Patsy Gallagher, Sandra Sorensen, Janet Stoody and Jim Harding, Gary Robins, Pam Hanna, Bonnie Currie, Walter Davis, Natalka Chomiak, Chrystia Chomiak, Sara Diamond, Jackie Larkin, Deirdre Gallagher, Shelley Acheson, Joan Kuyek, Larry Katz, Kathy Mugridge, Marilyn Keddy, Betty Lou Mills, Mary Morison and John Marshall, Ted Penney, Bill and Bobbie Gillespie, Nancy Riche, Kevin Quinlan and Marilee Pittman.

Not included in this book are about thirty-five women I interviewed. Each of their lives are important, unique and interesting. Each put themselves out for me, sharing not only their time and histories, but their homes and often their meals. Some picked me up from airports, rail or bus terminals, and later returned me. Though their stories aren't published in this book, these women helped to shape it, and their ongoing struggles in the workplace are setting the stage for a better life for their sisters and daughters at work. I salute them.

PHOTO CREDITS

Introduction

Work is at the centre of our lives. It provides the means of life itself, the goods and services essential to our survival and our well-being. Good work enables us to use our gifts, to develop our skills, to become proud and confident of our abilities. It fosters responsibility and cooperation among us, a sense of community with co-workers.

Few of us have good work by this definition. Yet it is something I think we all yearn for, consciously or subconsciously. At some level, the desire for good work is a major impulse behind women's workplace struggles, whatever form they take. The women who lead these struggles say about their work, as many of us do: "We want better. We want a decent living. We want reasonable working conditions. We want meaning in our work. We want human interaction and compassion. We want to use and develop our skills. We want recognition."

The women in this book have not stopped with the wanting, though. They fight for better. In so doing, they go against the feminine stereotype of passivity and subservience in the face of power. Yet it would be a mistake to mark them as extraordinary women, as especially intelligent, fearless or strong.

Few of us go to work with the thought that we will be catapulted into a struggle. The women who speak here are no exception. They work because they want to, because they have to support themselves or their families. They had few expectations — positive or negative — when they first took jobs.

The fact is that all kinds of women have taken up the fight for better work. Some dropped out of high school; others are university educated. Some are articulate, confident public speakers; others are painfully shy or solitary people. Some are slow to anger; others have a quick fuse. Many women are plagued by recurrent doubts about their own abilities, the sacrifices they ask co-workers to make, the possibility of making real gains.

Yet they persist, even though in many cases they fail to win the gains they seek. Ironically, it is in the struggle itself, rather than in the workplace, that these women discover their own special abilities, develop their skills and find pride in themselves as capable, worthy people. They learn to take the responsibility for changing things, begin to understand the importance of cooperation and the strength of community.

A few lucky women found, or created, jobs doing work they like in pleasant and stimulating environments. Workers at two cooperative daycare centres in Ottawa, for example, love their work with children, combining basic care with activities to stimulate the kids' development. They have eliminated competition and hierarchy in their work.

The staff are active in every aspect of the centre's operation: fund-raising, maintenance, the works. You feel that the centre is a part of you. You care about everything that happens to it. Plus there's the philosophy that all the staff — cook, coordinator, teachers, janitor — are paid the same wage. Our funders give us different amounts for each job, but we equalize it.

These workers are absolutely clear about the value of their work. But they still have to fight municipal and provincial governments for the funds to keep daycare centres open, to provide childcare so *other* women can work. Daycare workers, in common with other women, get very low wages for their work. Like women in other human service jobs, it was ingrained in daycare workers that they should subsidize the service. It has been hard for women in daycare work to demand funds for more and better centres *and* to make wage demands simultaneously. But they do.

Most women, however, begin their working life in the female job ghettos of service or clerical work. For some, the fight for better work starts with struggling out of these job ghettos. It's no easy task, as Cathy Mulroy found, and the opportunities are rare. She worked as a sales clerk and cashier for several years before the International Nickel Company in Sudbury opened its doors to a small number of women in a public relations ploy during Women's Year in 1975.

> Clerks, waitresses, bank tellers, behind the cash register, babysitting. It's the only jobs available for women in Sudbury. There weren't even real estate salesladies around at that time. There was nothing for women.

The options are bleaker still for native women in this country. The right and opportunity even to train for clerical work is circumscribed by the terrible effects of poverty and racism. Only the very strong make it. For women like Jessie Littlehawk, the struggle for good work begins with the struggle to get a job — any job.

> I remember the first day I went to secretarial school. I was very scared. I didn't have front teeth and I was wearing my only skirt. When I first walked in there I didn't know how I was going to last. When I looked at all these white women who seemed to be smartly dressed, the thought of quitting entered my mind. I wanted to go back to the reserve where I knew everybody. The thing that kept me going was that at the end of the week I was supposed to get a fifty dollar clothing allowance. After that the *Neheyaw* (Cree) in me got the fighting spirit.

Most women don't expect to need a fighting spirit to continue training, to stay on the job or to change the conditions of work. But then, few of them expect the aching discontent that grows out of the daily structure of their jobs. "It's a real assembly line," says a seafood worker, "rules and regulations for everything."

> Legitimate breaks are every two hours, right? And in between times you're standing on your feet all the time, doing the same monotonous thing. Thank God for sexual fantasies or you'd go nuts! If you're a person who can crawl around in your own head you're okay. But if you don't have an imagination, just to stand there all day without being able to think . . . It's loud, horribly noisy. You can't really have a conversation and keep up your quota. You can't tell jokes, you can't chew gum, can't, can't, can't, can't!

A mail sorter talks about the conditions which led her to be active in her union:

> I hated my job. I thought it was boring, it was stupid, especially after the advent of automation. I mean, here I was, just sort of shoving this mail into this little hole, and it just — went somewhere. I had never done work which was as dehumanizing, and to which my presence or absence as a person made no difference. At the post office, what was important was that my body was there.

Added to the mind-numbing boredom of these over-simplified jobs is the humiliation of petty supervision; having to ask permission to go to the washroom, "can raids" by supervisors, favouritism, constant criticism. A telephone operator says:

> You're never doing the right thing. I've been told I've been too friendly with my customers, too helpful in trying to find something, and then the next month told I was too business like; I wasn't spending enough time with them. So really, I don't think there's any time you can get a perfect record. There's always something that's going to be wrong with it.

For these women, work has become synonymous with soul-destroying drudgery. The work saps their sense of self-worth and robs them of confidence in their abilities. It becomes hard for them to imagine that work could be any other way, that women could actually change these conditions.

There is no single process which puts women into motion in the fight for better work. Some of the women in this book explain their fighting spirit as flowing from their personalities: "I resisted my mother all the way down the line as a kid." "I'm independent minded." "I'm stubborn." Others are encouraged by friends or co-workers who seem to be natural fighters. Loretta Burt, a squidjigger, says of her co-worker and sister-in-law, Betty:

> She pushes. I'm not that big of a fighter but she pushes me. She won't give in. And she got me in trouble like that a lot of times.

Together the women went to St. John's and then to Ottawa to demand the seasonal unemployment insurance that had been denied them and other squid jigging women along the north coast of Newfoundland.

Several of the women get involved in a workplace struggle almost by accident. Joan Meister, a clerical worker at Simon Fraser University, misunderstood what was being asked of her when she agreed to take minutes for her union's contract committee. She ended up bargaining with management through long and bitter contract negotiations and a major strike. A telephone operator, Debbie Sherwood, arrived at work just when the Telecommunications Workers' Union was beginning an occupation of B.C. Telephone Company offices. She stayed and it changed her life.

Still others take jobs with a conscious determination to make changes. Jeannette Easson and Debbie Field helped create the Women Back into Stelco Committee, which fought for production jobs at the Steel Company in Hamilton and won. Anne Bishop took a seafood processing job because she wanted to join the efforts of other workers to organize a union at Lizmore in Nova Scotia.

It isn't an easy decision for women to take up and continue a workplace struggle. The opposition comes from a variety of sources. Women first of all have to feel that they *deserve* better treatment, that they have a *right* to decent work. For some women these feelings don't come naturally. Gina Vance, a seafood worker, explains:

In this kind of area, a working-class poor area, a lot of women take rough treatment for granted. Like the women who come in all black and blue because their husbands, as they put it, "laid a beating on me." Women who are treated the way most of these ones are at home, well how on earth could they get the idea that you should expect something different at work? It's your lot in life to be done in by H.B. Nickerson. You don't expect anything else. You just give them your sweat and blood and take home your lousy little paycheque that you have to stand in line for every Friday, and just be grateful.

When women do overcome feelings of inadequacy or worthlessness, and seek better work, they may have to deal with the resistance of family members. Almost all the women in this book who do non-traditional jobs came into conflict with fathers or husbands. Cathy Mulroy describes the reaction of her husband to her work in the copper refinery at Inco:

He was threatened by my working with a bunch of men I guess. I never saw it. It didn't make any sense to me to fool around. I made more money but I don't think that mattered because it paid the bills. But I think the whole fact of my being independent probably scared him a lot.

Perhaps the most difficult struggle of all is to gain the support of co-workers. And for most women, this support is vital to making any changes at all. Yet the resistance among workers to upsetting the current order of things is founded on some very legitimate concerns. Gina Vance tells of the difficulties in organizing women seafood workers:

If you so much as mentioned the word union out loud it was very, very frowned upon. The women didn't want to make any changes. They were just thanking God they had enough work to get some unemployment insurance stamps for the winter. And a lot of them were single parents or had husbands who also did seasonal work. They didn't want to make waves. They were terrified they'd lose their jobs.

Fears of being fired are combined with common anti-union sentiments to create a formidable barrier against organizing in many work settings. Women in service work are particularly susceptible to the prejudice that unions are greedy and repugnant.

A lot of people in daycare are there because it's a nice thing for nice girls to do. To unionize is not nice at all. They were afraid that we would stop caring about the children and that we would only care about the money.

But the difficulties of activating women co-workers are not only ideological ones. The double day of women workers wears them down, makes it difficult to conceive of adding a meeting to the work day, much less take on a leadership role in fighting for changes. A seafood worker describes an average day in the life of her co-workers:

> (They) get up at three in the morning to make breakfast for a husband who's going fishing and then do their laundry and their housework and send their kids off to the babysitter's or to school and then put in an eight-and-a-half hour day down there and an hour each way travelling time, not knowing whether they might be stuck there until eight o'clock at night when they don't have enough food prepared ahead for dinner.

It takes a special effort, strong willpower, for women in these circumstances to get involved in changing their workplaces when the extra work will be so hard and the gains so uncertain.

Women who fight alongside men to improve workplace conditions may find invisibility to be a frustrating problem. Marion Pollack talks about the difficulty of being a steward within the Canadian Union of Postal Workers:

> As a woman I find it's a lot harder for me to be heard and listened to, and I've had to fight incredibly, and often obnoxiously, to be heard. I notice even now, when I'm sort of one of the leading people in the union, that I'll say something, and a man will say the same thing later and he's the person who'll get credit for it. It really pisses me off. Even when I have expertise in a specific area, people will not listen to me, they'll listen to the man, regardless of the fact that he's a new steward and doesn't know what he's talking about.

Invisibility, however frustrating, may be preferred to the sexual harassment that women face on jobs with men. Sexual harassment at work takes many forms. Relatively few of the women in this book had to deal with co-workers or supervisors who fondled them or coerced them into sexual liaisons. But many put up with frequent and degrading sexual comments and innuendo, derogatory sexual graffiti, or pornographic photos plastering the washrooms and lunchrooms. Contending with these forms of harassment was among the most difficult trials women faced with co-workers, because they were singled out for special treatment.

> We've put articles in our local's newspaper about sexual harassment. I wrote the first article. The day after the paper came out, every person on the floor had read the article. They saw "sexual" in the title and thought it might be interesting. And if I had never had sexual harassment before, after I wrote that article I heard every sort of comment and joke that was possible. I felt like going home and crying. It was just one of my worst ever days at work.

Downright hostility from men is a common experience for women who break into non-traditional jobs. In some cases male supervisors and co-workers directly challenge the right of women to "take men's work." Cathy Mulroy describes the reaction when she began work at the Inco copper refinery:

> "What do you think you're doing here anyways? This is no place for a woman. This is a man's job. Don't you know that you're taking away a man's job? A man has to support his family. And you're taking that away from somebody." And I'd think, "Well, maybe I am. Maybe I'd better start thinking about this." But then I'd think, "Well, Jeez, I'm supporting a family too. I'm here because I've got grade nine education and most men that work in Sudbury with that education work in the mines, so why can't I?"

In other workplaces the men have simply been incredulous that women are working in previously all-male jobs. In the coke ovens at Hamilton's Stelco plant, the men put new women workers through a difficult initiation.

> We'd go out there, and there's like ten males, two women, and we're shovelling, and sometimes you'd be trying to shovel through about two feet of coke off a track. It's a little hard to get your shovel in, and it takes a while to really know how to do it. And you'd look up and there'd be about twenty guys lookin' like they'd never seen a shovel, never seen a human being in their life before, just laughing and pointing and staring.

Animosity towards women in non-traditional jobs is not confined to the men they work with. Leni Balaban worked in logging camps, small confined communities where each person knew every other.

My social life wasn't the best. There were lots of families there, lots of wives, women in the kitchen, but none in the bush. It was again the typical one-horse town, the same bush camp mentality. The women were down on somebody who was a little bit different, who lived independently.

Ultimately, the fight for better work comes up against the boss. Sometimes the skirmishes occur primarily between women workers and their immediate supervisors. This is the case for telephone operators and postal workers. A mail sorter describes post office supervisors:

I think a lot of them are petty people, but also their power is petty, because in fact the only authority they have is the power to recommend discipline: they don't have the power to actually suspend anybody. So most of what they do is just very petty: being unfair, harassing workers, can raids, denying people overtime, not training people properly, personality clashes which the supervisors seem to go out of their way to provoke and continue.

At a smaller plant, the day-to-day conflict more often involves the general manager, who has more substantial powers. At Lizmore Seafoods, the manager "practices management by bullying. It's direct. Neanderthal." The plant is part of the H.B. Nickerson seafood empire, however, and at least among upper level management, a more modern approach has developed to keep workers in line. Says one woman of Nickerson's public relations director: "He's so congenial that you feel unreasonable when you stick to your position." Another describes labour relations at Simon Fraser University: "Things have gotten so smooth you can sometimes hardly tell one side from the other." Yet smoothness doesn't always hide an employer's contempt.

His first assumption is that he's working with uneducated, not very articulate women. And he comes in with his chummy approach: "Well now, Evelyn, we worked hard on this contract didn't we, and we're so proud of it, aren't we?" Between every line is written: "You are dumb."

Sometimes the struggle for better work also involves a provincial or federal civil service, either as employers or as administrators of work-related services such as daycare, unemployment insurance or workers' compensation. When four squidjigging women descended on the Revenue Canada office in St.

John's to find out why their unemployment insurance was held up, they were kept waiting for hours, then were told they wouldn't be seen. The women persisted in their demand to be shown their records and to be told whether they qualified for unemployment insurance payments. When they were finally admitted, one woman was treated to a bizarre test that would never have been given to a man.

> That woman from Twillingate, she qualified. She was going to get it. That was after they felt her arm. He didn't think she had muscles enough in her arm to be a fisherman, you know.

In another part of the country and in a different government office — social welfare — Jessie Littlehawk was worn down by contempt that took a different form.

> I finally left when I felt I could no longer live off the poverty of my people, getting a cheque every two weeks and yet not being able to do anything for them. I was really getting burned out. I was fatigued all the time. It was a real emotional strain to keep working there, especially with the bosses, who were mostly white men, whose attitude was that native people are lazy and were just trying to get a few dollars for nothing.

The fight for better work looks even more Herculean when women find that the boss, who seems to hold most of the cards already, has another power network to tap into. A small, autonomous union which represents university and college workers on the west coast had a look at documents distributed to university management during a national meeting.

> The universities have a national organization that stretches from coast to coast. They have lists of every single post-secondary institution in this country, broken down by whether they have a union, what kind of union, when was the last strike, how long did it last, what were the issues. They've got a national organization that is gathering together information that is going to help them fight us and win.

The more women learn about the forces opposed to improving their working conditions, the more overwhelming the fight seems. Yet few of the women in this book become so demoralized that they stop fighting. Sometimes the more opposition they confront, the more determined they become. And the moments of victory are sweet! Cathy Mulroy describes a showdown she forced on her supervisors at International Nickel when she called a meeting to register a harassment complaint:

> I had the upper hand. And I had them. For the first time in four-and-a-half years there I finally had them. You know when you go into a doctor's office or a lawyer's office, the phone is always ringing and they don't even say excuse me, they just answer it and talk while you're sitting there? Supervision always does that too. So I made three phone calls home to see how my kids were.

Women Back into Stelco won the right of women to work in the Hamilton steel plant with a hard-fought campaign.

> When I am a hundred years old, I will remember that we were capable of making Stelco jump — not only to our demands, but to our pace, you know? It really infuriated them that they were unable to take away the initiative.

Even so, the successes these women have had are partial, the gains they've made haven't come cheap. At Lizmore Seafoods the workers gained a union to defend their rights, but two years later the plant was shut down. Betty and Loretta Burt successfully demanded unemployment insurance for the Notre Dame Squid Women, but didn't get it themselves. Leni Balaban took on more and more challenging jobs in non-traditional work. Her marriage broke down. These women fought hard and made changes, but they find it's not possible to simply stop and enjoy them. Anne Bishop discovered that organizing seafood workers into a union marked only the beginning of struggle in her workplace.

> The lesson is that you just have to fight every single inch of the way. Fight, fight, fight, fight, fight. And meantime, it's as though the women in the plant are sitting back with their eyes narrowed, saying, "See, these outsiders can't do anything that we haven't done. See, you can't get anywhere with management." And what you need to counteract that is some immediate results. And you just can't get them. You're walking with your ankles bound in red tape every step of the way, and it's so very slow.

Still, it is not enough to measure success only by the advances in individual workplaces. Important breakthroughs happen at other levels. While the post office continues to battle ferociously against gains for women postal workers, the union is moving.

> One of the reasons we rejected the conciliator's report was because he didn't talk about paid maternity leave. The union leadership will follow it up because they're becoming aware of the power of women in the union, and they don't want to antagonize that power.

It's been a long fight to get existing union structures to take women's concerns seriously. It's hard for women to support unions when the discrimination that is a constant in most workplaces is also reflected in labour hierarchies.

> Women's issues tend to have low priority within unions, at convention. We had one just this week. Women's issues were last on the agenda. Sexual harassment, equal pay, technological change, occupational health and safety, especially as they affect women. The discussion was too brief, it was at the end, and we lost a quorum.

The support of unions for women's needs is built with a lot of effort. It's hard to know when and if there will ever be a payoff. But when there is, it's good.

> (At National Convention) we had a special meeting on the needs of women in the post office and in the union. It was really great. And one thing I was so proud of, every male delegate from my local attended, which means that a lot of the work we had done had really paid off. At a convention a lot of drinking and stuff goes on, and yet these guys all made the decision to come.

Changes in these women's personal lives almost always occur as a result of their fight for better work. Most important, they earn respect and admiration from family members and friends. Cathy Mulroy talks about the evolution in her father's feelings about her efforts:

> When I started at Inco my dad was totally displeased with me. It was no place for his little girl. But over the years he's been trying to fight the Compensation Board about his back injury and his hands. And now he talks to me about it. He calls and talks to me about the letters he got from Compensation.

A similar process occurred among the husbands of some workers at Lizmore Seafoods.

> One woman, the first time she signed her union card and her

husband found out about it, he ripped it into ten thousand little pieces. He didn't beat her, but he warned her that she was not to join the union, not to have any part of it. She is now the chairman of the health and safety committee. So there are changes happening in that direction although we still have to think hard to find them. The seed is planted.

The friendships which are forged in times of struggle are intense and intimate. Bonds which begin in workplace encounters often grow into longstanding personal relationships, women sharing the troubles and pleasures of both work and home life. These relationships give women the emotional sustenance and strength to continue in the face of sometimes overwhelming opposition. Leni Balaban speaks of friendships formed among several women loggers:

> I got a job working up at the Great Lakes Paper Company with eight other women in the bush camp — it was fantastic! I made some good and close friends that I'm still in touch with. I was operating heavy equipment. We all were. And I've never seen eight women that could stick together like that. An insult against one was an insult against all. We didn't take shit from anybody.

But perhaps the most profound changes occur in how these women come to feel about themselves. They take on tasks that few ever expected to do and they feel good about the abilities they've discovered and the skills they've developed.

> The strike was the best thing that ever happened to me, really. It brought me out of my shell. I found out who I was, that I can do things on my own. Jeez, I got a brain! I really do. I can learn. Because I only got to grade nine I never worked with numbers, and here I was paying eleven thousand people, helping pay them with vouchers.

Their experiences allow women to see the possibility of work as something different than daily drudgery. Telephone workers who occupied and ran B.C. Telephone offices in Vancouver for five days got a glimpse of another world of work.

> I went downtown and walked in and couldn't believe what I saw. All these people from my office were running everything. The positions were full. People were talking. It was more relaxed. At the same time there was electricity. The vibes coming off people, the auras around them were just vibrant, unreal. The people I worked with had seemed so humdrum, and here they were, _alive_.

Most of the women who tell their stories in this book were interviewed in 1981, and several of them continue the fight for better work in their workplaces. Others have changed jobs through a variety of circumstances: the Lizmore seafood plant shut down; Stelco laid off large numbers of workers, including all the women it had recently hired; the cross-cultural centre one woman worked in lost its funding; another left her clerical job at a university as her multiple sclerosis advanced; a daycare worker was hired as a service representative for a union. For all of them, however, the changes in their lives have been irreversible. Betty Burt, a Newfoundland squidjigger, speaks for them all:

> People are beginning to realize that they might as well come across, because women are going to fight to get what they wants. It's been a long time happening, out this way. People will say, "You don't deserve it," and we say, "Okay, we don't deserve it. We won't have it then, eh?" But now we're beginning to realize that we *do* deserve it as much as the men, and we're willing to stand up for it — I hope we are.

Jennifer Penney

UP AGAINST
THE ODDS

JESSIE LITTLEHAWK

SEVERAL PEOPLE HAD recommended that I speak to Jessie Littlehawk, an important figure in the struggle for native women's rights, an educator and researcher at a cross-cultural centre in western Canada. The image I had formed was that of a fiery orator. So I sat through a workshop the evening before our interview, not realizing the quiet, serious woman across the room was Jessie.

We met the next morning at the informal and comfortable offices of the cross-cultural centre. During the interview Jessie spoke very softly and slowly, pausing to search for precisely the right word or phrase, eyes often on her hands in her lap.

"We've always been told by our parents and our elders that we should not look people in the eye. It was disrespectful to stare at people when you talked to them. When an elder person spoke to *you, you were supposed to listen and have your head down to show respect. A girl was told that if you stare at a man, he might know some Indian love medicine and cast a spell on you. So when I moved to urban settings I found there were problems when I talked to people. I didn't understand until I realized that eye contact was considered to be very important, especially when you talk to social workers, the police, when you go to court."*

I AM FROM the Plains Cree Nation. I was born in a tent on a reserve in northern Canada. My grandmother is a midwife and she delivered me. I have five sisters and five brothers. I am really the fourth oldest, but one of my sisters died of double pneumonia when she was three months old, so now I am the third oldest.

We lived in a one-room log house. We only had two double beds. My parents slept on one bed with the baby, and five of us would squeeze into the other bed, while the rest slept on the floor. Many mornings we would wake up to find the water frozen in the pails, and the bannock frozen. My dad would make a fire and put bannock in the oven to thaw out. The hot bannock was delicious with lard and a little bit of salt.

There were no day schools on our end of the reserve, and the government said we had to attend school or have our family allowance cut off. So we had to go to a residential school away from the reserve. I started school when I was seven. It was a girls' school run by the Anglican Church. I still remember getting physically sick because I was lonesome for my family. I would be sleeping and hear my mother coughing. I would wake up abruptly and then find myself on the top bunk. I would see rows and rows of double bunks.

One of the things I remember about my experience in the residential school is how my hair was always cut. There were times when I had lice, but there were also times I didn't and still they cut my hair. Now I am growing my hair. It feels good to have power over my hair. No one will ever cut my hair against my will again.

I used to look in the staff's garbage cans. I used to find toast, and I would eat it because toast was a luxury. We never had toast in the residential school.

I used to get good marks in school. There was a prize of five dollars to go to the student with good marks. I was well on my way to getting it, but my peer group started fighting me. They didn't want me to win the prize. They must have been jealous, but anyway I surrendered. I gave up under pressure. I deliberately wrote wrong answers and played dumb. I had no big sister to take my side. My oldest sister had dropped out of school and my second oldest sister was in the sanitorium with tuberculosis.

White guys used to come to the school to pick up Indian girls. My friends and I used to sneak out at night. We would return to school just as the sun was coming up. I met a white nineteen-year-old man who I felt I sincerely loved. I guess he didn't. I became pregnant at fifteen.

I had to go home and face my parents. They had such high hopes for me to finish school and be a nurse. Now I was a failure. My self-image hit rock bottom. I felt worthless.

My oldest son was born when I was sixteen. I loved my baby and took care of him. He was very beautiful. I lived with my parents and sisters and brothers in a two-room log house. They all loved my baby Robert. They all helped look after him.

Being young I started getting restless. I started drinking. I hung around skid row which was the river street. During that time there was a song that was popular on the country and western hit parade: "Squaws Along the Yukon Are Good Enough for Me." The message I was getting was that I wasn't valued very much.

I found myself pregnant again. I was very upset. I didn't want to shame my parents again. It was at this time that I met my husband. We are from the same reserve. We used to drink a lot. I got it into my head that I could blame him, make him believe that I was carrying his child. That's how I became involved with him, because of this obsession that I could not shame my parents again.

I had a miscarriage and lost the baby later on. By that time we'd lived together and I wasn't able to get out. I had to get a

"Mrs." in front of my name, so people would see me as decent. I thought if I could get this man to marry me, we would separate anyway. But it didn't work out that way. When we married he really felt that he owned me, and because of that, the marriage lasted fifteen years. It was very stormy. We had numerous separations.

He almost always had a jalopy. In the spring and summer we used to go to the beet fields of southern Alberta. We looked forward to going after being cooped up on the reserve for the long winter months, and because there was no employment on or near the reserve.

I got pregnant again with my youngest child. He was born in the beetfields in Alberta in 1968. We came back to the reserve in the fall.

I quit drinking when I had my baby, but my husband didn't. I'd be home with the children and be terrified about what would happen when he got home. And I asked myself if it was going to be the same story for the rest of my life. I couldn't look forward to another five, ten years of the same thing.

We lived on social assistance, which at that time was ninety-seven dollars a month for two adults and two children. It wasn't even a cheque; it came in the form of a purchase order.

I left the reserve in February 1969. Our assistance at the beginning of that month was almost all gone and I didn't have any wood. I didn't have any winter boots or mitts to go out in the bush and cut wood. So I went next door to my parents' to sleep there for the night. When I got back the next morning the two water pails had frozen open. I decided I could not depend on anybody but myself.

I moved to an urban centre. And I guess because I had completed grade eleven, I was fortunate in being able to go into business college. Otherwise, Indian Affairs wouldn't have helped me financially and I wouldn't have been able to leave at all.

I left with my two children and went into a boarding house situation where Indian Affairs paid my room and board. We had one suitcase and one cardboard box which held our worldly possessions at the time.

I remember the first day I went to secretarial school. I was very scared. I didn't have front teeth and I was wearing my only skirt. When I first walked in there I didn't know how I was going to last. You know, when I looked at all these white women who seemed to be smartly dressed, the thought of quitting entered my mind. I wanted to go back to the reserve where I knew everybody, my parents, my family. The thing that kept me going was that at the end of the week I was supposed to get a fifty-dollar clothing allowance. After that the Neheyaw (Cree) in me got the fighting spirit. To quit meant to give up and I absolutely refused to do that. So I stayed.

By that time my husband had followed me and was staying at the Salvation Army Hostel. He also started going to school, upgrading classes. The counsellor at Indian Affairs told us that if we got together and found our own suite or house, that they would pay the first month's rent. But when we went looking for a place, they'd have the sign in front of the house "Suite for Rent", and I would go and ask to rent it. They would say, "We don't rent to Indians" and slam the door.

We did find a suite, but a few weeks later my husband quit school and started drinking again. He and my brother, who was babysitting for us, would drink together. They would bring beer up to the suite after the bars closed. I would not get to sleep till about two or four in the morning, and then I had to get up and go to school. I fought and pleaded with them not to bring liquor to the suite. I threatened to go to the police. I lied to them, saying I had gone to the police and that the landlady had threatened to kick us out if they brought liquor again. The drinking did stop for a while.

I completed the secretarial course in December. It depended on the individual the rate you went. One of the subjects we had was spelling, which was easy for me, so I was able to write the final exam and get it out of the way. And this went on with the other subjects like typing and shorthand and bookkeeping. So I got my diploma from there and was able to get a job in the Department of Natural Resources.

The Liberal government at that time was setting up something called the Indian and Métis Department, a kind of affirmative action program where they were trying to get native people into government agencies like the Department of Natural Resources. So it was through them that I was able to get this job in the office. I was being paid by the Indian and Métis Department.

Looking back now I can see that it was mostly a "jane job." I typed, answered the phone, did filing, took shorthand from the boss.

Later I got a job at the Department of Social Services, where again I was being paid through the Indian and Métis Department. I'm sure that if I had gone as an individual to apply for work there just on my own merits, I wouldn't have been able to get it. They were just not hiring native people. A lot of people who worked there had B.A.'s. And I didn't have any contacts at all.

I was an assistant welfare worker. It was mostly chauffeuring for the social workers because they wanted to devote their time to counselling. Later on I was offered a position as a worker for single women with children. I was to contact the woman and provide her with social assistance if she needed it, and if she was placing her child for adoption, to prepare the social history for the court.

One of the things I was happy about when I worked with Social Services was I felt I was really making a lot of money: $389 a month. The secretarial job was $250 a month.

But also at the same time I was having a lot of marital problems. The Department of Social Services required of its workers that we attend tri-regional conferences. The first one was held out of town. But my husband was very angry when he found out I had to go for three days. He didn't really say why, but he just got very angry. When I went there he kept phoning. I could tell he was drinking. He would start crying on the phone and say, "What are you doing?" And he put my youngest son, who was four years old at the time, he put him on the line and he would say, "Come home."

Another time this male social worker was leaving Social Services and was going to transfer some foster homes to my case load. So one day we drove out to the country where he was going to introduce me to the foster parents. I knew we were going, but I didn't tell my husband because the worker was a man. We left about nine-thirty in the morning and were back by five. My husband was supposed to pick me up. He didn't come, so I started walking home. I met him on a street close to home. He told me to get inside the car. As soon as I got in he started swearing at me and saying, "You bitch!" And he started hitting me. He drove to a back alley. He kept on hitting me, but I opened the car door and jumped out. So somehow he had found out that I had gone with the male worker. I went home and he didn't come home until after midnight. Of course I couldn't sleep. I was too scared. When he got home he started accusing me and I had to run. He was trying to hit me and I had to duck and run. It was in the winter so I wasn't able to run out. I guess I could have if I put my winter coat on, but I didn't want to leave the children.

I felt very guilty, that I was to blame, that the fault was all with me. I was ashamed. I never confided in anyone. Once, when I was on emergency detail, I had to go and make a call after supper. When I got home he threw a cup at me, with a spoon in it. The spoon cut my eye. The next day I went to work with this patch. And I didn't tell anybody about it. It was a very painful time.

Another Indian woman was working there. She missed some work and then would come in with visible bruises. She would say she got into an accident. But the two of us were native women and I know we were experiencing the same problems. We could not confide in each other, tell each other what was really happening. I guess at that time, I felt it was a very private, personal problem.

I heard the social workers talking about battered women that were on their case loads, as if the women were masochists, as if they did something to provoke the beatings, as if they loved the beatings, saying if they didn't love it they would obviously leave the situation.

I guess at that time I also noticed that a lot of people receiving social assistance through the department were of Indian and Métis ancestry. There were many families who social workers referred to as "protection families," families that are having marital problems, alcoholism and social problems. I started asking myself a lot of questions about why this was, what was happening in my life.

In August of '72 we moved to a larger city so I could go to university. I had never heard about university until I started working at Social Services and heard all these workers talking about sociology, psychology. One of my old teachers sent me a newspaper clipping about the mature adult admissions program to the university. I didn't have to complete grade twelve. So that's when I first knew I would have a chance to get in.

My husband didn't mind moving. In the town we'd lived in I had laid charges against him for battery and withdrawn the charges. So we were getting known. The people we knew, our families, knew all about the problems we were having. I just wanted to leave that behind and maybe make a fresh start.

I enrolled in Arts and Sciences. I was taking a B.A. majoring in anthropology. I took a lot of sociology classes. Well, it wasn't difficult for me. They have such big rooms and the professor lectures. I really enjoyed it, you know? Hardly missed any classes.

I didn't have time to study at home. My husband wanted a clean house, and of course housework was my responsibility. I couldn't study. I should talk to him instead of reading. He would give me a lot of negative criticism about myself. I never was able to read the textbooks. I used to manage by attending lectures and doing the required essays.

The daytime classes I didn't have any problem with, but a sociology class I had to take was only in the evenings. That created problems with my husband again. He didn't like me going to school at night. He would be waiting for me, angry.

At that time too I had the rest of my front teeth out. They were aching. I'd never heard about root canal treatment. They never told me about it. So I had to go to school without teeth for seven weeks.

My tuition was paid, and books, and I was given a living allowance which was $162 every two weeks for a woman with two children. But I could not always depend on my husband. What he made was his. He would help with the groceries, but the rent and other bills were mostly mine. He'd buy clothes for the youngest but not for my oldest. I couldn't really depend on him. He wasn't always around to help. Even though he worked, he lost a lot of jobs because he would go off hunting. He wouldn't tell them at work that he was going. He would always end up drinking. Sometimes he would be gone ten days.

At this time I was a heavy smoker. I smoked first thing in the morning and last thing at night and even during the night. Since I did not like roll-your-owns but only the tailor-made cigarettes, smoking was expensive. The training allowance was not much to live on. I wanted my children to drink juice and milk. I decided to quit smoking so I could buy them for my children. The first three days were very hard. I sweated, I cried, my head ached. But I was determined to quit and I did.

I used to love to go to the university bookstore and look at the books. One day I saw *Reservations Are for Indians* by Heather Robertson. I devoured it. It was the first book I had seen and read about us. Then for the first time it began to sink in, what had happened to us, the Indian people. Before this I used to think we were poor because we didn't try hard enough. At the same time I knew I certainly worked hard and still I was poor, and I could see many of my own people working hard and still they were poor. I used to think that some day when I had a degree I would make lots of money and I could get a job any-where. By the time I finished reading *Reservations Are for Indians* I knew what had happened to us as a culture. I cried a lot at that time. Especially when I would be reading and I'd remember what I had heard from the elders, the stories my father and great-grandfather had told me. We had been a proud, happy people. We had our own everything, our own tribal law, our own education system, our own extended family system, our own religion. We believed in the Creator, the Great Spirit. We had worshipped God in our sun dances which we used to attend every summer. We had our own recreation and sports, our own economic system which were the buffalo.

I joined Urban Indians, a group of treaty Indians from the reserves who we met in the city. You know the government funds people on the reserves. But when you leave, you don't get the money anymore. What was happening was that people wanted to buy a house. It was impossible. So we were trying to get some of the money that was provided for housing into the city so that people could be assisted to buy homes. And trying to get the chiefs and the federation of Indians to recognize us. A lot of them felt that it was our choice to leave the reserve, and once we did, we no longer existed, we had no rights. In the city, Indian Affairs will keep us for one year, provide social assistance and then refer us to the provincial government. Yet nobody really wanted to have anything to do with us. The Urban Indians were trying to at least get recognition, and also there was a lot of education to do.

I got my degree in 1975. Then I went to work for Indian Affairs. I actually started with the feeling that I would be able to do something. Another thing was that when I was a student and had to go and get my cheques at the office, I once heard one of the workers there telling a person in the waiting room, "You lazy son of a bitch. Why don't you work instead of trying to get welfare all the time?" I felt that if a person like that could find work there, then I could. At least I wouldn't do that to people.

At first I was hired as a student for the summer. There weren't any vacant jobs. I was training on the job and being paid by the Indian and Inuit Program in Ottawa. I thought that having a degree and being a native person I would be able to get a job very easily, but it took me almost two years to get a permanent position.

I had a lot of curiosity. I wanted to find out what they were doing, what power they had over me as a treaty person, and also I guess I really hoped that I would be able to at least provide social assistance to native people who couldn't find work. It didn't work out that way. I used to give assistance. I just used to hand it out. It was forty dollars every two weeks for a single person who couldn't find work. But later on even that wasn't possible, even though there weren't any jobs.

One day I told a supervisor what I thought. I told him I believe we live in a rich country with a lot of money. It goes into things like nuclear development. I said that there's no jobs here. I felt people have to eat. I said I was going to give assistance, at least the basic assistance to people who couldn't find work. We live in a rich country. Why are some people hungry?

Well, he said that jobs were there, and if people really wanted to work they could.

Most of the social workers are white people. I used to see people if there was an emergency. But what the white workers wanted and required was that people have an appointment. And we were so booked, one solid week in advance, because there were only two of us for the whole city. When I would see people without an appointment, the front desk reported me to the district manager, and I was given a talking-to.

Once the CBC wanted to interview me about the kind of services we provided for people who leave the reserve, so I went to the head boss and he said yes. But when they came in, a lot of the staff really.... They told the crew to leave. But the head boss said they could stay and we closed the door. I guess the staff were scared about what I was going to say. Like, some of the cheques I had tried to make. I'd pass the decision sheet to the clerk who was supposed to make a cheque, and he wouldn't make the cheque. A lot of them they just didn't accept.

I finally left when I felt I could no longer live off the poverty of my people, getting a cheque every two weeks and yet not being able to do anything for them. I was really getting burned out. I was fatigued all the time. It was a real emotional strain to keep working there, especially with the bosses, who were mostly white men, whose attitude was that native people were lazy and were just trying to get a few dollars.

When I started working for Indian Affairs I had started night classes for my social work degree. By this time it was almost done. It took me three years of night classes and some Saturdays. I never worked as a social worker after I completed my degree.

I started at the cross-cultural centre in September. We provide a resource centre, do workshops and teach courses on social issues. I had other jobs I could have taken. One was with a native women's organization. We had our first meeting a year ago. Some of us had been involved in things individually as native women but not as an organization.

Other organizations were already in existence. Urban Indians was set up by some of the men, and the Indian-Métis

Friendship Centre. I attended other women's organizations and really enjoyed them, but I felt that we really needed our own group, our own time to get together, to get to know and relate to each other, being women and native and single parents. I feel that within any oppressed group many identify with the oppressor and not with themselves. Also, we live such a hard life, one that other people don't know about. Our lives are filled with crisis. Our children go to juvenile court, adult court. Not having enough money to live on. Being battered women. And now even some of our children are battering us. I know a woman, I saw her just this morning, her head was big bumps where her son hit her. These are experiences that a lot of people never go through. So we want to start not only seeing them as personal problems but social problems, that in our system the poor get prison.

We need a home base, you know; our daughters especially need role models. Just telling them they can do it after years of socialization to the contrary is not enough. They have to see it.

We are the first generation of women who are leaving the traditional role. I know what it means to be called a squaw. It conjures up an image of a dreary drudge, doing all the menial work, a slave to her husband and eager for the affection of any passing white man. I know that feeling of having no confidence, feeling inferior. And I know it has a lot to do with my being a woman and a native person. Many of us possess such negative self-images. We experience the stigma of having a brown skin and black hair in a white culture. It is not just inside our heads, it is a reality.

One of the worst forms of racism and sexism is that of omission. We as native women are not there. In glancing through the new history books I was beginning to feel,   Ah, it's not bad; I don't feel put down or ridiculed, at least. But after a moment's pause I realized it was because we as Indian women weren't there.

I try to be assertive, but sometimes I get tired of adjusting and having to cope. I get tired of having to fight for my human rights. I'm in line at the Dominion Store with a white person behind me and the clerk chooses to wait on the white person. If

I'm tired I'll just let it pass. If not, then I'll say, "Sorry, I was here first."

I feel sorry for native men. They could no longer go hunting when we were put on reserves, while we women still had the domestic duties and childcare. To be successful for a man is to have a job such as a minister, teacher, carpenter, mechanic or supervisor, but these jobs are not open to all men, especially not to Indian men. But all men can dominate women. Most men have physical power. For years Indian men could only vent their rage on Indian women. We are aware of why our men are frustrated, because of unemployment, racism and discrimination. We also suffer and are going through the same hell. Why take it out on us?

What we women do is to internalize our anger. It comes out in getting drunk or depression or obesity or suicide. We need to work our anger out through energies, having meetings, setting up our own schools, trying to change the basic structure of education. To see the problem as the education system and not within our children.

Things are better for me now since I separated from my husband. I don't live in fear. I can go to meetings at night, I have more freedoms like that. My financial situation is a little better too, since I can now control my money; it doesn't go to him. But there's still problems. My children have had contact with the criminal justice system. I hate that. They are twenty and fourteen. My oldest son was first in jail when he was sixteen, and almost every year since. He's going to court again next month. My youngest is going to juvenile court this afternoon. He's still in school but he misses a lot. He doesn't like it.

This is a good place to be. I'm kind of protected here. I'm not always fighting discrimination, racism. If I worked at the Human Rights Commission, for example, checking complaints of people being discriminated against in employment, in housing, in going into public places, I'd have to fight it for myself. It would always be in my experience. Here I don't have to, not in my work.

We are a collective. When we have staff meetings we decide things together, like whether we will respond to requests from groups to speak. Native women who have been involved here have often been exploited, being asked to go and speak. I realize that sometimes we were cheap entertainment for church groups: it made them feel better if they had a native person to talk to them. But they were not really committed to doing anything further.

Here, being involved with our union, I'm finding out more about the basic rights of a worker. This is the first time I'm working in a place where the conditions are good. I've had it so good here. I have parent leave, for example, so I can take time off this afternoon to go to court with my son. I've been able to talk to women that I work with about some of the things we just don't have to accept. They are people who have known their rights for a long time, people who are assertive and are used to standing up and fighting for their rights. That's something new.

I really want to learn more here, to get a real grasp of our system, to be able to make that clear when I talk to people. I can translate into my own language, Cree. I want to be able to describe in Cree the system we live in and how it touches every part of our lives. We have to work with other groups, to support unions and women and native people, people in Third World countries, before we can have a victory. They suffer too.

Native people think that all white people have it good, that you are all rich. That you all go on holidays, are all materialists, that you know all these things. But that's not true. Seeing the films last night about child labour, about people who had no homes, didn't have enough to feed their families, I realize that other people suffer too. We have to work with them. I'm glad I recognize that, but the stereotypes we have of each other get in the way.

I put up a sign in my bedroom that says: "I swear it to you, I swear it on my common Indian woman's head: the common Indian woman is as common as a common loaf of bread . . . and will rise!" I look at it whenever I get discouraged, and when I really get depressed I chant it. Sometimes I do a lot of chanting. It's a great sign. What's really great about it is that it says the *common* Indian woman. All of us. Not just the exceptions who finished high school or who got married at the right time, but every single one of us will rise.

JESSIE LITTLEHAWK is a pseudonym for a Cree Indian woman living in western Canada. When the cross-cultural centre she worked for lost its funding, she went back to work as a social worker for the government.

*S*eafood workers Gina Vance
and Anne Bishop at Lizmore Seafoods,
Lizmore, Nova Scotia

NO LOBSTER FOR LIZMORE

GINA VANCE
&
ANNE BISHOP

GINA AND ANNE *are relative newcomers to Nova Scotia. Gina moved there from Jasper, Alberta in May 1977. Two months later she was hired by Lizmore Seafoods, where she worked for the next three seasons. "It was instantly noticeable that there had to be some changes made. It was just so oppressive, rules and regulations for everything. You weren't allowed to smile at the person beside you without somebody glaring. I'd never worked in a situation like that before."*

Anne first met Gina when she was working for the People's Food Commission, investigating the food industry in Canada. When Gina started to organize the plant workers into a union, Anne helped from outside, and later was hired to work at the plant herself.

Anne explained that the Lizmore plant was owned by H.B. Nickerson and Sons. "They have close to a monopoly on seafood in Nova Scotia. That means that when they threaten to close down a plant if the workers don't toe the line, it's not an idle threat. And unemployment is so bad here, you can understand why people don't stand up for themselves."

Two years after organizing the plant, and still under the threat of a shutdown, Gina and Anne talked with me. It was a rainy Thanksgiving day. Gina's husband, Robert, replenished the coffee cups as we talked through the hours.

GINA: For three years that plant was my whole life. Getting it organized, making a better opportunity for the people coming in after me.

You work for the season, however long it lasts. This year it was only ten weeks; they didn't do any crab. But my first season was six months, six days a week, nine, ten hours a day. We started at the beginning of May and worked right through to the end of October.

It's a real assembly line, rules and regulations for everything. You couldn't smile at the person beside you without somebody glaring.

The lobster are live when you start. At least they're supposed to be. Inside the factory they go through a cooker first and there's chemicals added to the water, and then they go to a break-off table where Anne works, where you pull off the tail and the body and the claw sections and they're all distributed to various tables in the factory. And the production workers then proceed to pick the meat out of them. Then they move down the line to be washed and canned. Then stored, either hot packs or cold packs, and shipped to whoever the buyer might be.

The tails are shipped to the States, to restaurants. You can't buy them in Nova Scotia. You have to get the whole lobster or nothing.

During the season you only get Sunday off, but even Sunday is geared towards the factory because of washing uniforms, aprons and gloves. You have the stink of the plant with you everywhere you go, the whole time. And people in the streets literally back away from you if you don't change your clothes, 'cause you really smell terrible. You come home and you've gotta wash all this awful stuff out, and get it outside so it doesn't stink up your whole house. So even your time off is centred around going back there. You never get away.

ANNE: I was living in a cabin this summer that had no running water. So Sunday I'd get up early to haul my water to wash my uniforms. And I had an oil stove that didn't work all the time and I'd try to cook my food ahead for the next week so that I didn't have to face cooking when I got home, whenever I got home every night. So Sunday I'd get up early, spend the morning doing the wash, the afternoon cooking ahead. It gives you Sunday evening to yourself, and I'd try to get ahead on my union newsletter on Sunday evening. And then Monday morning you're back into it again.

GINA: It consumes you. You have no time for anything else. I cannot fathom how women with two, four, six children, and husbands who do nothing but lay around and drink, how they manage. It's beyond my capabilities to function in that situation.

ANNE: And those who get up at three in the morning to make breakfast for a husband who's going fishing . . .

GINA: . . . and then do their laundry and their housework and send their kids off to the babysitter's or to school, and then put in an eight and a half hour day down there and an hour each way travelling time, not knowing whether they might be stuck there until eight o'clock at night when they don't have enough food prepared ahead for dinner. And to stand in that wet, cold environment all day, doing the same thing over and over and over.

ANNE: The monotony. You use all your ingenuity to think up things to do to keep from going up the wall. And the noise! You're standing just a few feet from the women next to you, but if you try to have any conversation you have to shout, and pretty soon you just get worn out. It's the machinery. There's the cooker, which hisses except when it's being filled up, when it goes *ka-bang!* (Laughs.) *Ka-chunk, ka-chunk, ka-bang!* The boiler goes *psssst*, and the vacuum pump makes a horrendous clatter when it comes on. I couldn't even begin to imitate it. The metal conveyor and the cooling tank constantly rattle. And the lobsters coming off the end go *chunk-chunk-chunk* into the stainless steel break-off tank. And those awful pumps, which blow up every now and then, come on with a roar and then cut out suddenly. Your ears are left buzzing for hours after getting out of there. But the big thing it does is to cut you off from the women around you 'cause you can't keep up yelling for too long. You have to go into your own head.

The thing I was grateful for this season is that I was on a non-quota job.

GINA: She got really lucky. She got chummy with the boss and got on a non-quota job. (Laughs.)

ANNE: It's a non-quota job because the conveyor coming out of the cooling tanks sets your speed. Sometimes you have to just madly scramble. And other times you know you're getting towards the bottom and it's slowing down. Then you get a walk every now and then. You fill up pans and carry them to the weigh table. That's the highlight of the day, that little walk to the scales.

GINA: All the years I worked there I was under constant pressure to meet my quota. I'm not the quickest person in the world, and it was tough for me. I really had to work at it. For some people, if there wasn't noise they could carry on a conversation and still put out fifty pounds with very little effort. It took a lot of concentration for me.

ANNE: You're a left-hander that they tried to turn into a right. The line is set up for right-handers. In crab, the quotas are the same for everybody. Everyone gets a whole body with all the legs on it and the claws. You're shaking the meat out of the body, you're snapping off the legs, cracking the claws and picking them. Everybody's doing the same thing. Everybody's got the same quota. You don't get money for going over your quota. You just get fired if you don't meet it.

GINA: You just have one general pile of meat and it all goes in the same stew. In lobster you have fifteen different sections.

ANNE: You have people cracking claws and people picking thumbs and people picking arms and people pulling tails and people cleaning tails and people running legs through the wringers. The wringers are awful. One person got her hand in it this year and one person last year. They're like washing machine wringers only they're steel and there's no release mechanism on them. There's a stop but no release. So when a hand goes through there, it has to come back out the way it went in, which is a real drag. No guards. We fought for guards this year but haven't got them yet.

The other thing that really gets to you is standing on concrete in rubber boots all day. I put thick work socks and felt fillers in my boots and that helps. A lot of people don't use them, though I don't know why, 'cause it really gets your back. And I can't imagine going through a pregnancy in that place, though lots of women do.

It gets your legs, just everything in you starts to hang down. It gets your digestion. My system got all fluey in there.

GINA: Plus nothing's geared to the individual. Like the tables are all high, so a short person has that much more difficulty.

ANNE: On the break-off table you've got a stainless steel tank that comes up to just above my waist. I'm one of the taller women, so leaning over that, two feet down, is something I can do. You have a rake about three feet long, and I'm the only one who could reach all the way across the tank and pull the crabs towards me. The shorter women on the break-off get a severe pain in their shoulders and down their backs from that reaching, reaching, reaching, but I can do it just fine. Whereas the tables where they pick were way too low for me. I found myself scrunching down, or standing on one hip. And I ended up with hips that still ache if I walk too much in a day. In the cold you shiver. On a hot day, when you've got steam coming out of the cooker, you get cooked. (Laughs.) Anywhere else you freeze because of the cold water running over the floors.

GINA: And your hands are in cold water. My hands will never be the same again. The minute they get cold they go numb on me. I used to wake up half a dozen times at night and it was just like your whole hand's asleep. The last season I worked there, when

I was killing, we used to have to start sometimes at six. The killers would start early to get the crab in the cooker before the main factory opened, so the women would have stuff to work with. And I would have to get up earlier and run my hands in hot water and exercise them so I would have feeling in them by the time I got to work, so I could do my job properly.

ANNE: Still, weather like this, I wake up with my hands all swollen and sore.

GINA: And it will never go away. I've missed the whole season this year — I was working someplace else — and it's still there.

ANNE: It's a great place to work, real fun. (Laughs.) The main thing is the monotony and a sense of meaninglessness. A lot of the lobster that goes through is rotten. There wasn't much that went through this year that I would eat myself. So you have no pride in your product.

GINA: Some people couldn't get through a day at Lizmore without a joint at noon. In fact, there were a lot of people who smoked before they went to work in the morning, who smoked on break, who smoked at dinnertime. I wasn't one of those people, but there were a lot who used it to blot themselves out, to get that quota. Some people can really go when they're stoned. They can really work.

ANNE: Maybe religion used to be the opiate of the people. Now it's booze. And grass. And television. But mostly booze and grass. (Laughs.)

I only tried it once. I accepted a toke and didn't make my quota that afternoon. At that point I was still on probation; it was my first month on the job. I was known as the editor of the union newsletter and I could not afford not to get my quota. So I never did it again. Still, it was a fun afternoon. I had this wonderful sensation of floating two feet above myself, watching myself work and saying, "Now why is she working so hard?" (Laughs.)

How did the union get started?

GINA: My first season, H.B. Nickerson (the parent company) incorporated something they called the "committee" in the

plant. It consisted of three people who were supposed to represent the worker to management, to identify problems and say,
"Okay, we'd like you to do something about it." At the end of my
first season I was elected to this committee.

At first I thought I really could do something. I even went so
far as to write up pages and pages of stuff for David, the plant
manager, showing him how to make improvements in conditions which would eventually improve production as well and
save money for the company. I figured that would be the clue. If
I could show him how he would make money at Lizmore, then
he would be more willing to make changes.

I would speak to him on the phone about something, and he
would encourage me to write it down. But then it would get
dumped in his garbage can, unopened I'm sure.

The committee was made up by the company *for* the company. And we had no real voice whatsoever. If we said, "We'd
like to have toilet paper in the washroom," well, you could say it
all you wanted, but there'd never be any. We'd say, "We'd like to
have a fifty-cent raise," but if you got a nickel you had to accept
it. What recourse did you have?

David was using us to do all his dirty work, too, anything he
didn't want to do or couldn't handle. Like, people wouldn't show
up for work on Saturday. He'd tell us it was *our* fault. We were
supposed to control that. He'd say, "It's your job. They're workers just like you, and you've got to tell them that they're going to
get written up, they're going to get a legal warning. They may be
suspended. You must see that these people show up Saturday
and Monday." Which were the two worst days. He was putting
all the shit on the committee.

After a while I just sat there and shook my head. "This is
going absolutely nowhere." It festered all that winter, and I was
thinking of not even going back. But you sort of get revitalized
during the off-season. You sort of begin to think, well, just
maybe, just maybe. . . .

Evelyn Anderson and I sat in this very room with a bottle of
vodka one night and decided to start a union. Evelyn had been a
shop steward for a union when she was at Electrohome, before
they left Nova Scotia. Her husband is a fisherman, so he phoned

up some people that he knew and Evelyn was given the names of two different unions. She called one number and got no answer, and she called the other number and got an answer. And that's how we ended up in the union we're in, the Canadian Seafood and Allied Workers.

The national president of the CSAW came up to meet with her and left her union cards and basically explained what the initiation fee would be and said that once we got our percentage of cards filled out to call him back.

We had to wait until the season started again because we had no other way of contacting people. We had no phone lists, no addresses. The only ones we could contact were the ones who lived in our own little area, that we knew personally. However, if you so much as mentioned the word union out loud, it was very, very frowned upon. The women themselves were anti-union. They didn't want to make any changes. They were just thanking God they had enough work to get some (unemployment insurance) stamps for the winter. And a lot of them were single parents or had husbands who also did seasonal work. And it was their livelihood. They didn't want to make waves. They were terrified they'd lose their jobs.

ANNE: And scared to go on strike. Everybody thinks if you join a union, you've gotta go on strike.

GINA: If you go on strike, you've got no job, you've got no money. The plant will close.

During my first season there I found out who was pro-union and who wasn't, and out of a hundred workers there might have been six that were pro. You sort of glommed onto them and said, "Okay, help me." (Laughs.)

Anne wasn't in the plant at this point. But we had become friends, and she was very supportive. I would get so discouraged and Anne would say, "Hell, don't quit now. Hang in."

We'd go around the plant whispering in the course of working or going to the washroom. Sometimes you were in situations like at the break-off table, where you have a whole group of women. You would just casually start a conversation: "How do you feel about getting a union started? We didn't get a raise last summer. This might be the ideal way to get one." "Are you happy with your working conditions?" — whatever you could squeeze in. We got a lot of negative reaction, but surprisingly we got a lot of positive reaction too. Management was going through a phase when they were giving us a lot of hassle. So women were getting more readily worked up to it.

We talked about working hours, overtime pay, Saturday pay, general working conditions. Enough heat in the cold months, some fans in the summer, just day-to-day comfort things like toilet paper, clean toilets, not having proper conditions for washing up.

ANNE: Washing up on company time. Scales.

GINA: Being able to weigh your meat in at the end of the day without having to stay over and not get paid for it. Like, you're not allowed to leave your table until a buzzer rings at four-thirty. And at this particular point, when you have between eighty and a hundred people and only one weigh scale, somebody gets out of there half an hour late. And it's on your own time. So we started sneaking into line about twenty-five after four. And for two or three days we would get away with it, but after a week or so — boom! The first ten people in line would come in the next day and their time cards would be docked a half-hour's pay. Well, it was stuff like this going on that made organizing easier.

Management caught on to our activities very early. They did nothing. David thought it was a great joke. In the beginning he'd meet me in the hall and just grin at me from ear to ear, as much as to say, "I know you're trying to organize, honey, but I got you women under my thumb; you aren't going to get anywhere." Later on he started to get worried and went around threatening people, especially the fellas working out back, the boys. "You can't join this union. If you do, you're out of a job." And that made their backs come up all the more.

The big job was convincing the packing table. They're the elite of the plant. They've all been there many years, and a lot of other people pick up on them. So once we got one or two packing table workers behind us, they sort of fed the rest of the plant. And it looked really good.

We had a meeting where the national president came in to a local hall in Lizmore. This was after the union cards had been signed but before certification. And it was a huge turnout. And though it wasn't cut and dried, we felt, from here on in we have a union. That was my moment of glory, to be backed up by all those women, and I felt really good about it.

But then we found out we had to have a vote. We'd got seventy out of ninety-five workers signed up, and you shouldn't have to have a vote with such a large majority. But the company claimed they had three-hundred-and-some employees. You see, everybody's laid off at the end of the season, but they're still registered as workers in the plant; they simply don't come back.

ANNE: A Lizmore worker never dies. (Laughs.) Your name stands on the list forever.

GINA: So the Labour Board came in and decided we'd have to vote. And it was to be done in the office with the plant manager sitting there glaring at you.

The day of the vote, everyone was geared up for it. Evelyn and Margo and I and the other people who were gung-ho went around whispering in people's ears, "This is our big chance. We're going to do it. We're going to pull it off today. Vote with us. If we stick together we have a chance."

When the Labour Board fella came, I was the first person out of the plant to go in and vote. And by the time I had begun the procedure, there was ten people lined up behind me. We were so excited.

ANNE: I phoned up Gina that night and asked, "What happened? What happened?" She said, "I don't know. They took the votes off to Halifax." She was sure they were going to lose because you had to put your vote in an envelope and write your name on it. And people were convinced that they'd know who had voted which way.

Well, none of us knew anything about this. So I called someone who has had some experience with unions and asked why, and he said, "That's because they decide who's eligible to vote *after* the vote." The company and the union argue in front of the Labour Board about who qualifies to vote and who doesn't. Then they pull out the envelopes of the ones who aren't eligible. Meantime it's a wonderful trick to scare the people who are voting. It's hard to convince them that the manager won't know how they've voted.

GINA: While we were waiting for the results, people were starting to change their minds. They were scared. There was no information. They thought this waiting period had something to do with Nickerson putting pressure on David to close the plant. And all these rumours started springing out that there were not gonna be any crabs, that we were going to shut down, and the union, the organizing, was all to blame. And it all came back on Evelyn's and my heads.

ANNE: The union was giving out *no* information. Since then, I've asked the national president about unorganized plants in the Nickerson empire. He said, without thinking, "Oh, there's a couple, but they're less than a hundred workers. They're not worth our while." That about sums it up.

GINA: Three weeks after the vote they sent us a letter. We had won, fifty-five votes out of sixty-eight. We put the results up on the bulletin board, but feelings were already going the other way. Management was waiting for the teeniest mistake to just jump on somebody. Things were very tense. And women were thinking, "Gee, maybe we did the wrong thing here. We were better off without this hassle. We should have let well enough alone." There was absolutely no sense of victory. Nothing.

David was told to watch, I'm sure, for any little thing that was against the rules, bring it up the very first thing, make an issue out of it. He was sneaking around corners, watching people.

There is a rule, although it was non-written, that you are not allowed to eat the product. It's not your product, it's the company's product. You do not eat the lobster, you pick them. Well David's version of this rule was: "Eat it if you want to. Just don't let me catch you." (Laughs.) He used to walk around with his mouth full all the time. But that was different. He was management. It's *his* product.

So, twenty-five after four one fine Friday afternoon, a co-worker, Betty-Ann, is weighing the meat, and she's working at a table directly across from what we call the wringers, where you put the large leg through from the crab, and the meat comes out nice and whole in one beautiful piece, right? It's the best meat on the crab. Betty-Ann's walking past the wringers and there are two legs just laying there, not doing a thing. (Laughs.) So she puts them through the wringer, and she has the meat out of both of them, one tucked in her mouth, chomping on it, and the other ready to go. Well, there are people all around going to the scales, and it was the end of the day and David was watching. She turned around and she caught his eye, and she knew right away that she'd been caught. He didn't say anything to her. He went back to the office and told one of the lead hands to send her into the office. Well, she was suspended for a week without pay for eating that crab leg. And the end result of that was she was one week short of her stamps for unemployment.

It happened at a time when people had been stealing salmon by the whole fish and getting caught and not being suspended for it, or fired or anything, just having to cover it out of their pay.

Then one of the lead hands decided to take the side of the girl who ate the crabmeat, and organized a walkout. They called up the television station. They called up the newspapers. This was all independent of the union. But she definitely thought the union should support her.

So I called our national president to ask what we should do and he said, "Stay out of it. There's nothing you can do. You can't help her. The union can't help her. It'll mess up contract negotiations so bad that you won't get a nickel. Stay out of it."

It looked very bad for us, very bad. We were unable to do anything. The executive felt it had to listen to our national president. We didn't know that we had any other choice. He was the man who was supposed to know. He'd been in the job for eight years. He'd worked in a fish plant for twenty-five before that. We were looking to him for guidance. But he wouldn't come anywhere near the plant when it was going on. Not anywhere near. And he told us to stay out of it. If the newspapers came, not to make any comments. If the TV crew came, to stay inside the plant, to make sure all union executive stayed on the job, because if there was going to be a walkout it would be illegal, and the union could be fined for the loss of production for however many hours or days they stayed out.

So we got to work at quarter to eight this one morning and Betty-Ann is there with her following and the TV people are on the way. And the union people crossed the line and went into work.

I guess about an hour and a half later everybody came back into work. But there was a division right there between the union and the production workers. Everyone came down hard on us for not helping her, that it was a cop-out. And as far as we were concerned, it was. All set up by the company. It was perfect for David. He was just waiting, and we walked in at the right time.

ANNE: It was lesson number one about how the union can end up being the police in the plant. Because Betty-Ann had quite a legitimate complaint. David had just had a row with the fella that Betty-Ann lives with — he's a fisherman out of our harbour — and there's a lot of suspicion that David suspended her to get at her boyfriend. She was legitimate to be angry about it. It was very unjust, arbitrary treatment like everybody gets around here. But the union gets caught in such a funny position.

GINA: Right. We were going to unify the workers. We were going to be a union body and support each other, and here's the first case of the workers getting shafted and no support, not an iota of support.

The phone rang here every two minutes for two days and two nights. I think the neighbours reported me to the telephone company, because we're on a party line. Everybody was phoning: the people involved, the other workers, forelady, everybody. "There's gotta be something you can do for Betty-Ann." "I'm trying, I'm trying. I don't know what to do. I'm trying to find people that do know what to do." "Anne, help!"

ANNE: You should have heard the phone calls from Gina. Oh, my God, it was just horrible. She'd call and she'd say, "It's all over. We never should have tried it in the first place." (Laughs.) The phone call when Betty-Ann walked out with those thirty-seven people. . . . I worked in the Toronto Distress Centre for four years and it still stands out as one of the most depressed phone calls I ever received in my life.

I was still working outside. I had applied for a job in the plant that March but didn't get hired until August. Meanwhile we were consulting by phone and seeing each other after work, and I was doing some running around, helping to find out information, get a lawyer, things like that. I was wringing my hands that I couldn't get in there. They were signing the cards and going through the hassles around certification. Then, finally, about two weeks after they were certified, I was hired. Here I was thinking, Oh, I missed it, I missed all the excitement. (Laughs.) And I got in there just as the shit began to fly. (Laughs.) We were so green. Somehow we thought that when you were certified that was it; you were home free.

When I started, things were very tense. I had to continue being just as quiet as I had to when I was outside the plant because I was on probation for thirty days. I wasn't protected by the union at all. Management can fire you like that (snaps her fingers) when you're on probation. So I had to support Gina without being seen myself.

GINA: Fortunately, Anne quickly caught on to the type of work that goes down there and had no trouble meeting the quota. Had she not met her quota, then it would have been out the door and up the hill.

ANNE: As a matter of fact, when I walked in the door there the quota was twenty-four pounds in an eight-hour shift. But within a few days it went up to thirty pounds. As a new hand I was struggling to make twenty-four. When I made it I was so proud of myself. And it went up to thirty. And then, when the union newsletter started coming out, with my name on it, they put it up to forty. It went from twenty-four to forty within three weeks.

GINA: First, and they hadn't done this before, they threatened us with the quotas. They fired at least two dozen people for not making forty pounds a day.

This is conjecture on my part — I have no proof — but I think that Nickerson came down on David and said, "Look. You let this happen. You ignored it. You thought it was a joke. Now get on your toes, boy, and do something. We've got to get rid of this before anything else happens here." So they brought in Vanderballs.

ANNE: His name really is Vanderval, but we called him Vanderballs. (Laughs.) He was an efficiency expert sent there to straighten out Lizmore.

GINA: All of a sudden this guy was stalking around the plant in his white hard hat, watching everybody. Then, out of the blue, he called a staff meeting. He took us all upstairs on our lunch break and informed us that the hourly non-contract cigarette break we were having would be cut out. No more. They're not in writing; we're not allowed to have them.

Well, for those of us who smoke, of course, it was a horrible situation. Legitimate breaks are every two hours, right? And in between times you're standing on your feet all the time, doing the same monotonous thing. Thank God for sexual fantasies or you'd go nuts! If you're a person who can crawl around in your own head you're okay. But if you don't have an imagination, just to stand there all day without being able to think . . . It's loud, horribly noisy. You can't really have a conversation and keep up your quota. You can't tell jokes, you can't chew gum, can't, can't, can't, can't!

So you're just sort of dying to go for a pee and a puff. But there were people who abused it, non-smokers as well. Especially the summer staff, the school kids, who were a very different breed from the woman who was there supporting her child or children, making a living for herself and hoping like hell that the job was going to last long enough for her to get unemployment during the winter months when there would be no work. The school kids loved being able to sit up in the lunch counter area and while away twenty minutes. So Vanderval had a point. But his whole attitude was: "I am God. And this is the law. And you will do this. There are no questions asked. There are no questions answered. You have been told and that's it. There will be no discussion."

ANNE: His speech was priceless. "Ladies." (Pause.) "Ladies, I'm concerned about your production." (Pause.) "Your production is going down." Well, we knew our production wasn't going down because our secretary-treasurer was on the canning machine, and she was telling us how many cans were going through a day, and it was more than ever before. "Your manager has been very good to you. He has given you these breaks. But I am his boss and I feel that it's a little too much and I have to take these breaks away from you." (Laughs.) "It's for the good of Lizmore Seafoods," he said at the end, "and if you don't like it, you can find another job." As if there's any other job for women in this area.

GINA: "... and I'd like to be the first one to know which job you find that gives you five breaks a day. I'll go to work there myself."

ANNE: He left us seven minutes for lunch that day. I counted.

GINA: And lunch takes you ten minutes to get settled into because we have no place to eat. We eat in our cars or on the beach if it's nice. We have no official change room or lunch room.

ANNE: The pressure was on. The things that people had been getting away with were cut off. They made it compulsory for the first time to ask permission to go to the toilet.

GINA: And you could only go twice a day or you had to bring a doctor's certificate.

ANNE: And you couldn't be there for more than five minutes. They brought in this warning form about not meeting your quotas or going to the bathroom too often or being insubordinate. If you were "disobedient," you were called out and had to sign a form in the presence of the foreman and the lead hand.

GINA: The women were terrified. They were coerced into signing, told that if they didn't sign the form, it was an admission of guilt. And they didn't know any different. They were out there crying, especially the young kids. They were promised that at the end of the year it would be wiped off their record. But they had to sign.

I got one myself. It was just foolishness. They just wanted to take a union representative and drag them out into the hall and make sure everybody knew about it. They said I was being "insubordinate" because I was going to the washroom four times a day. I said, "How am I being insubordinate? I ask permission to go." Well, of course neither of our Betty's, our two lead hands, had had to deal with this shit before. They didn't want to turn anybody down, so they always said yes if you asked permission to go.

Well, this little talk happened just after lunch. I stayed in the plant until about ten to four, which was about my usual time to go for a smoke. I went up to one Betty and asked permission to leave the plant. I was refused. Went to the other Betty and was refused again. They both said, "Gina, Clarence (the foreman) told us we're not allowed to let you out. We have to go with it. It's not a personal choice." I said, "Okay, find Clarence for me." I must have waited ten minutes. I wasted three times as much time going from one Betty to the other and waiting for Clarence than I would have if I had just routinely gone for a smoke. Finally, Clarence came. I said that if I wasn't allowed to leave the factory, I would just have to pull my pants down and do it in the middle of the floor. (Laughs.) He just sort of stood and glared at me for about twenty seconds. Finally he backed off and said, "Okay, go if you have to. Don't take any longer than necessary."

ANNE: Our manager practises management by bullying. It's direct, Neanderthal. (Laughs.) He's just so obvious. But apart from the hassle about bathroom breaks, they changed tactics. They brought in this foreman from the National Sea Plant in Caribou, and he claimed to be pro-union. He was a real sweetheart with the women, acted like a son to some of them. He'd sit down and listen to a problem, say, "Yes, that's terrible. We should do something about that." He had no power to change anything, but it worked. Word started to spread that now we have this foreman we don't need a union, because he's so good and sweet and gives us everything we ask for. What do we need a union for?

When they took away the breaks, that was blamed on the union. Then a group started passing around a petition to get the union out of the plant. They got fifty signatures out of ninety women that were working at that time. Fifty signatures. We were going crazy because we didn't know if they could decertify us or not. We thought, Here we've been certified for three weeks and we're already down the tube. So we were in a mad scramble for information. We found out they couldn't decertify us for a year, but it still scared the pants off us.

GINA: And this petition thing happened during the three-day period that the union executive was away at negotiations, so there was no one to defend the union. I was vice-president, so I was gone.

ANNE: That was the peak of the anti-union feeling in the plant. And that's what brought me out of the woodwork. Because none of the three were in the plant, and nobody else would stick their neck out. (Laughs.) So probation or no, I had to come out. Just at that time I went to a meeting where I talked to a couple of long-time community organizers and they said, "If you can't get them any other way, you've gotta use humour. They can't fight humour." And they suggested starting to draw cartoons and put them up on the inside of the bathroom cubicles, just to poke fun at all of this. So the next week we really got moving. We bought this potty and wrote around it: "For those who have to go more than twice a day" and put it on the wall above the time clock. Well, even the foreman thought that was funny.

GINA: It wasn't much of an issue after that. But what really ended it was a shutdown threat by the health department. The plant had been ordered to clean up in three days or shut down. Everybody got involved in the clean-up, really put in an effort because it was getting close to stamp time, eh? Just one, two stamps away from getting money during the winter months. We wanted desperately to keep the place open. So we all chipped in.

ANNE: People worked together until midnight. One night Gina and I and another woman were the only ones left and we were laughing and carrying on, having a good time.

GINA: Everything was concentrated on the clean-up, and the washroom thing just flew out the window and has not been an issue since.

ANNE: Still, union work was a real effort. We couldn't get people out to meetings. They were ashamed to come because they'd be seen as pro-union. And for women who work a fifty to fifty-six hour week and have children at home, meetings are a hardship anyway.

GINA: And people travel from as far as Rushford and Antigonish, an hour and a quarter away. It's a long trip for them, and trying to find a central meeting place is tough.

ANNE: So everything was sort of falling apart, and we realized that what was happening too, is what so often happens. There was a little drama being played out between the company and about four workers, five at the most. And the rest of them didn't have a clue about what was going on.

GINA: And they did their best to keep us separated from other people so we couldn't really share the information at work.

ANNE: The rumours were growing up and the insecurity was there because there was no information. And if you can't give them information via the meetings, then you have to find another way. So that's when we invented the newsletter. We used it to communicate to workers, to give the information and debunk the rumours and do our cartoons. And that was our turning point.

It started as a one-page mimeograph. We sat up late at night writing and typing articles and drawing cartoons. A church in town agreed to run it off.

The first week we distributed it Gina was at another negotiating meeting, and I had to give it out all alone. I'd go around to the cars at lunch hour, and they'd glare at me through the glass and I'd say, "Do you want a newsletter?" (Laughs.) And they'd roll down the window two inches and I'd stuff the newsletter in apologetically (laughs) and they'd glare at me until I went away. Nobody wanted to be seen reading it. Some people got vicious about it, crumpled it up in front of me and tossed it at my feet. It was like handing out leaflets at a demonstration or something. People would mutter "communist" at us. Well, communist is the worst insult around here. (Laughs.)

We called it *Our Very Own Rag*. It created a bit of a scandal. Like, "rag" to me has always been a slang term for a newspaper, and it was a word Gina and I used between us when we were thinking about putting together a newsletter. We discovered later that a rag is a used Kotex in rural Nova Scotia east. (Laughs.) I didn't realize what was going on for a while. I didn't realize what people were upset about. It's gotta be changed. People are still scandalized by it.

But people read the newsletter. It's about *them*. By the second week those car windows were coming down. It was the last three weeks in the season; we printed one every week. By the third week we didn't even have that much to say, but people were asking, "Is there going to be one this week?" And that Friday noon hour, they followed us out to the car and near swamped us. Out they went like hotcakes.

GINA: We reported what was going on in negotiations. Not that we were getting anywhere. It was a complete disaster. All you have to do is take a look at our contract and you'll know how badly we did. (Laughs.)

Our executive met at a local hotel with our national president, Lawrence Wilneff, to draw up our contract proposals. He brought a contract from another plant and said, "Okay, this is all basic union stuff. We'll incorporate all that into your contract." We had no idea what he was talking about. We spent the whole day going over the contract clauses. "This is what the company will want, and they'll ask for it and we'll put it in." There was no input from the members about the union demands. None. Absolutely none.

In negotiations there was David, the plant manager, and Fred Bennett, labour relations manager from Nickerson, on the other side. For us there was Lawrence and our executive: president, vice-president and secretary-treasurer. Management sat on one side of the table and we sat on the other, and never the twain shall meet.

At the old company "committee" meetings, Nickerson's used to buy us lunch, and we'd bullshit about the weather and how many cans a day we were putting out. But in negotiations, labour sat on one end of the dining room and management made sure they found a table where you couldn't even see them, never mind communicate about anything. There was a clear separation: you are on that side of the fence and we are on this side of the fence.

ANNE: You have to actually be in negotiations to believe how management operates. Our own manager is such a bully, such a crude, stupid bully, that he's very easy to counter. You can be just as stubborn in return and it's fine. But with Fred, the labour relations manager for Nickerson's, it's different. He's very, very smooth.

GINA: He's well trained, there's no doubt about it. He used to be a plant manager himself, for General Mills. Nickerson's is small beans for him.

ANNE: He knows exactly what he's doing. He's perfect for them. And he knows he's dealing with women. The reason I was so good at dealing with him at first is that his first assumption is that he's working with uneducated, not very articulate women. And he comes in with his chummy approach: "Well now, Evelyn, we worked hard on this contract, didn't we, and we're so proud of it, aren't we?" Between every sentence is written: "You are dumb."

GINA: If he thinks you might be just a little bit above these inarticulate, dumb women, he'll try to flatter you. Things like: "Gee, you've got a lot of smarts, Gina. If you ever decide you want to work higher up in the Nickerson Corporation, there's a job in my office for you."

ANNE: He's so congenial that you feel really unreasonable when you stick to your position. The last time I was dealing with Fred it was over a grievance, and we were going to hold out. And I held out and held out and held out through a half-day meeting and a couple of phone calls. I just kept saying, "Fred, we want this." After I'd been standing at an outdoor phone booth for over an hour talking to him, I just wanted to finish. But he would just talk and talk and talk and talk, and repeat things over and over and over. We'd been through the whole thing at least five times. And he was refusing to acknowledge my points and just kept repeating his, and repeating them and repeating them. And it was all on our local's bill, and our local had about $100 total. And I just wanted to end the conversation. Finally he said, "Now, Anne, you seem like an intelligent, reasonable sort of person. I just don't understand why you're not easier to get along with. We should be able to co-operate on this." Well, I stuck to the demand. But inside I simply folded. All my courage, my determination, my pride at how we'd dealt with this grievance for months and months, just went phht. Crumpled into a little heap. That's the longest I've held out against Fred's tactics, and he still got to me.

GINA: It took us all the next winter to even get management to talk money at all, or anything to do with money, like health. We have no sick time, no sick leave with pay, and if you hurt yourself at work, that's it, you're off without pay. If you can't get compensation or unemployment insurance, you just don't get any money. So we tried to incorporate a health plan, with them paying so much and us contributing so much. Well, that was money, and they would not talk money. Period. Any proposal that had anything to do with money was shafted to the end of the line 'til it was so close to the plant opening the following spring that they were going to have us over a barrel. They just kept hashing and rehashing issues that could have been settled in no time at all.

We were just at a stalemate. Finally, near the end of negotiations, management offered us ten percent, but they wanted the right to drop any person who did not meet their quota for each work week back to three dollars for that week. That was the minimum wage then. They wanted us to agree to that! The only reason they threw it in there is they knew we would fight it tooth and nail, and that would become the major issue. They used it so we would forget about all the other issues and just settle for having that removed from the contract.

It worked. We took the ten percent, took the money. No one was up for a strike at that point in the season. Unemployment was running out. The wages went from $3.50 to $3.85. Without the union we would have got 50¢ in two years. With the union we got 35¢.

GINA: The big lesson of the negotiations was that the contract doesn't always say what you think it says. It can seem very self-explanatory and explicit, but once they get their lawyers working on it, you realize it's like a sieve. It gets reinterpreted. Everything is ambiguous, and they turn it around to suit their own purposes.

Even union deductions. The company agrees to deduct union dues from the paycheques, but then further down it states you have to sign a card to give the company permission to take this money off.

ANNE: And you can withdraw your permission at any time. Talk about contradictory! There's been no one that we've gone after, specifically and individually, and asked them to sign the permission cards that has refused. But in two ten-minute breaks and a half-hour lunch every day, how many people can you get to sign cards? We fell behind on signing the permission cards simply for lack of time. Consequently, their dues weren't deducted and we lost a lot of money.

Another example. On the wage chart it says the lead hands will be paid twenty-five cents more an hour than the highest category supervised. Well, there are several fellas out back at the end of the plant who get the male salary of $4.50 an hour. Management didn't want to pay the woman lead hand $4.75 an hour, so they took the men out from under her supervision and put them under a fella who worked at the wharf, who doesn't know what goes on in the plant. The fellas out back feed the lobster into the cooker. You have to keep an eye on them in order to have the fish go through at an even rate, so you don't sometimes have fifty people standing around doing nothing. The lead hands got caught in this position where the fellas were horsing around and they couldn't say anything to them and the fellas knew it. The lobster wasn't coming through. We were sitting there twiddling our thumbs, and then the lead hands would get shit at the end of the day about the number of cans that were put up. There was nothing we could do to fight it because the contract isn't specific enough to prevent this kind of discriminatory interpretation.

We're keeping a list of things that need correction, that need clarifying. We'll probably miss some. But what I've learned is you have to think about each clause as if you're a lawyer going into a grievance. And you have to assume that management will get whatever they can out of that clause.

Working under that contract this season was really hard. I ended up back in the plant, but Gina had left for another job. The past president and past secretary-treasurer had lost interest. I felt like a one-woman union. I *was* a one-woman union. (Laughs.)

GINA: The way I felt before you came.

ANNE: Exactly. But it was so different the year before when we were both at Lizmore. I was living here at Gina's. We travelled to work together. We travelled home together. We were at work together. And boy, talk about a situation in which you can learn from each other, reflect together, that was really exciting. When

Gina wrote me during the winter and said she'd taken this other job and wasn't going back, I almost didn't come back myself.

GINA: It was tough for me. I felt I *should* go back for all those reasons. On the other hand, I felt it was time to do for Gina. I had given all I could. I wanted time to rethink my own self, to become a person within myself, removed from Lizmore. I needed a job that was going to give me something more than a paycheque, where I wasn't constantly consumed.

ANNE: I felt there wasn't a lot I could do alone. I ran off the newsletter for the first couple of weeks, but there was no support. Call a meeting and thirteen people show up, and them not very interested. What a drag! And there were so many things that needed to be fought. The manager was just stomping all over the contract, stomping all over the workers, arbitrary as usual. For the first time the working conditions really got to me. I discovered how fifty to fifty-six hours a week of standing on concrete, doing something monotonous, can wear you down. (Laughs.) It really did. I was just dripping tears into the break-off tank and nobody cared. (Laughs.)

I remember Gina saying after certification, "Oh God, I can go back to eating lunch." I felt the same way this season. When you're working there you *need* your ten minutes morning and afternoon, and you need your half-hour lunch. But before I could get any dues coming in, I had to get all those permission cards signed. Same as during certification. So I was spending each break trying to get one or two people to sign and each lunch talking to three or four. You spent the time doing that. You didn't eat, didn't sit down and have your tea. It just wears you right down.

The shop steward at the beginning of the year was terrible. I discovered afterwards that people had been coming to her with legitimate complaints, and she was saying, "Aw, why bother? You can't get anywhere with it anyway." Things were bottling up like a pressure cooker, and I was too tired to psych it all out.

And I'm an outsider. Both Gina and I were. That's part of the reason there was resentment against us. It's also why we could imagine things being better. We're not Maritimers, I'm not married, and neither of us have children. We speak differently, have more education, all that. It meant I wasn't getting wind of this stuff. And the pressure was building along with the old notion that the union's useless and it was hopeless to fight.

I finally realized that the shop steward was feeding into all this, and I was trying to think of a way of sacking her. It would have been tricky, but then she had to go off for minor surgery. I said, "Well, why don't you take this all off your mind and resign as shop steward?" (Laughs.) And she did.

It was coming around time for elections, and both Evelyn and Margo said they didn't want to be executive any more and I said, "Fine. Just help me come up with some people to run for the new executive and I'll let you off every other hook." (Laughs.) And Evelyn did. She came up with Sharon Roberts. And talk about one hell of a super shop steward. Energy! She has her ear to the ground.

GINA: And she's married, too. To a real Maritimer.

ANNE: And she's got children and she speaks like a Maritimer. And she has no education. She's worked in factories all her life and she's splendid! All of a sudden there was somebody else. And the whole thing picked up.

Sharon and I work very well together. I'm very cool. I walk in like a lawyer's apprentice with my homework all done and tucked neatly under my arm, but I'm very sensitive about the non-rational thing. You know, being brought up in a liberal, university-educated household, where if I threw a tantrum I was carted off under my mother's arm and told to stay in my room until I was more reasonable — that stuff. And it works to a certain extent, never getting into a flap, being cool. It can be very powerful. But then there comes a point to explode, and Sharon does it. Like, late in this meeting over a grievance, Sharon hadn't said much before, but she just blew her cool: pound, pound, pound! And it was just the right moment. And it was the thing I couldn't do.

So all of a sudden there was some support, some leadership coming forward from real working-class Nova Scotian women, not us fakes. (Laughs.) Sharon found another person, the woman she works beside, very, very quiet. When Sharon first said, "I think she'd make a wonderful secretary-treasurer," I was a little sceptical, 'cause she'd never opened her mouth. But Sharon talked her into running and she's turned out to be just ideal.

And next we had a health and safety committee of three people. It worked beautifully. It was a place to put people that were beginning to show some leadership and wanted to do something but weren't quite executive material, or their husbands wouldn't let them. And the three we put on the health and safety committee really got a lot out of it. First they managed to get some steps fixed. Then they tackled a really serious problem.

The floors are washed with sodium hypochlorite every night. There are acid compounds around that get on the floor, and that means you're breathing chlorine gas for the first two hours every morning, and your eyes water and your throat stings. They managed to get the foreman to hose off the floors half an hour before we walked in every morning. It was our one big visible accomplishment.

But the big battle for the year was that the manager wasn't taking us seriously, and he was doing the same thing he used to do with the old company committee. We'd come in and say, "We want this, we want that." And he'd say, "Oh, of course, I understand. We'll do something about it." And nothing would happen.

So we started to put in grievances. This was all new to us. We were flying by the seat of our pants. The first one was over getting back pay for an experienced worker who was rehired and had to go through a probation period again. We got an agreement to give her her back pay and published it in the newsletter. Well, she never got it. So we put in this grievance. David didn't take it seriously. We waited the twenty-four hours for his response, which was supposed to come in writing. There was no response, nothing. So we told him we were going to take it to arbitration. We had to give him written notice of arbitration before twelve-thirty that day, in order to legally go ahead with it. David went out to the wharf and climbed on a bulldozer.

Evelyn and I followed him out. We trailed him around the wharf in our little white smocks and little truck stop waitress hats, our aprons and rubber boots, waving this paper at him while he trundled along on this bulldozer. (Laughs.) We shouted, "We have to give you this sheet before twelve-thirty." "Take it into my office. I'll be there in a minute." "We have to give you this sheet before twelve-thirty!" We knew he'd claim he didn't get it. "Take it into the office. Can't you see I'm busy?" "David, you are accepting this from us now!" I finally held my apron and uniform back and leaned over the tread of the bulldozer and stuck it in his hand. There was no way he could not take it.

He was supposed to respond in forty-eight hours. No response. So we named a lawyer and we named an arbitrator. The president of the union complained to us, though not too strongly. He didn't like the money it would cost. He wasn't happy about this at all.

GINA: Union elections were over for two years and Lawrence, the president, was safe with his several thousand dollars a year raise. He didn't need our little local any more. And he wasn't about to spend any money that was unnecessary on poor old Lizmore. But on the other hand, he couldn't exactly say no. But he tried to dissuade us from going to arbitration. We ended up doing a lot of things on our own, without him, as soon as we knew proper procedure.

ANNE: In some ways he wasn't very happy about the newsletter either, because we criticized him. (Laughs.) But he didn't want us to go to arbitration.

We explained to him that we had to make the manager start taking the contract seriously. We named our lawyer and our arbitrator. The company had ten days to do the same.

Then Lawrence called Fred Bennett at Nickerson's and apologized for us taking it to arbitration and offered to talk it out. Fred asked Lawrence to suspend the whole procedure until he could get down here to meet with us and negotiate the griev-ance. Lawrence agreed without consulting us, which annoyed me but there wasn't a lot I could do about it. So we met Fred. I told him, "If you don't get back to us on this in forty-eight hours, we set the whole arbitration in motion again." He was really upset about that, got all huffy.

Well, Fred basically got David off the hook, by offering to give the grievor her back pay from the fourth day after she started, which was when she began making her quota. It was a pretty good settlement as far as she was concerned, but we realized that it changed the whole meaning of probation. It usually means a thirty-day block of time, after which you're a qualified employee. And now he's saying she gets full pay from the first day she's made her quota. So we said, "Okay, then. Probation has never been understood this way, but we'll settle on condition that we can look through the records of everybody who started this year and see what day they started making the quota." "Oh no! How many more people have you got in the woodwork?" says Fred.

It ended up in a battle over seeing the quota charts. They finally gave us access to them. It took us two full days to go over the charts. Susan, the bookkeeper, walked in while we were doing it and asked, "Did I do something wrong?" And just to tease her I said, "Oh, yes, your charts are all screwed up." (Laughs.) Well, she's the most conscientious person you can imagine, and she went away really upset. Later we found out that Susan had already gone through all the new employees' records, and Fred was making us redo the work.

It turned out that three other employees had made their quotas long before the end of their probation, so now we're submitting another grievance on behalf of the three of them. We'll see where that goes. But the lesson is that you just have to fight every single inch of the way. Fight, fight, fight, fight, fight.

And meantime, it's as though the women in the plant are sitting back with their eyes narrowed, saying, "See, it's useless." "See, these outsiders can't do anything that we haven't done." "See, you can't get anywhere with management." And what you need to counteract that is some immediate results. And you just can't get them. You're walking with your ankles bound in red tape every step of the way, and it's so very slow.

One of the difficulties of working with these women is that most of them are married to a man, or live with a man. So first of all they have their housework on top of their regular work, and they can't get out to meetings. The men don't lift a finger about the housework. And in this kind of area, a working-class poor area, a lot of women take rough treatment for granted. Like the women who come in all black and blue because their husbands, as they put it, "laid a beating on me." Women who are treated the way most of these ones are at home, well how on earth could they get the idea that you should expect something different at work?

GINA: It's your lot in life to be done in by H.B. Nickerson. You don't expect anything else. You just give them your sweat and blood and you take home your lousy little paycheque that you have to stand in line for every Friday, and just be grateful.

ANNE: My suspicion is that the reason we succeeded in organizing here is a particular combination of being on both the inside and outside. Gina and I were outside enough to be outraged by the plant but inside enough to be able to get inside their heads and figure out how to say things and adjust our language and not be like a union fella at the gate handing out leaflets. Women just don't respond to that.

GINA: We were there, doing the very same damn thing that they were, hour after hour.

ANNE: And making the same money was really important. We were making $3.50 an hour too. The only difference was that we didn't have children to go home to. I would love to do more comparing notes with people who work in textiles and restaurant work, because I don't think you can organize from the outside. You run into certain problems in an industry that has a majority of women in the workforce that you wouldn't if you were working with "the head of the household." (Laughs.)

Women feel *guilty* if they cause any trouble. And the husbands reinforce this by saying things like, "Now don't you make any trouble down there and lose your job." A lot of the husbands are anti-union. If the woman doesn't support the union, you can talk to her directly, but if her husband doesn't, you can't talk to him, you don't know him, you don't have access to him. If he doesn't support your union, she can't.

The reverberations of organizing go home. And you don't even know what they are unless you know the woman personally, what kind of hassles she goes through at home or what kind of hassles the union is causing for her. If a woman wants to take more of a part in the union and she shows up two days later with a huge swollen black eye, then I start to question what the hell I'm doing. Maybe I should just shut up my mouth. I guess this is something that organizers in a basically male industry just wouldn't face.

GINA: We're making some inroads; some of these husbands are coming around. One woman, the first time she signed her union card and her husband found out about it, he ripped it into ten thousand little pieces. He didn't beat her, but he warned her that she was not to join the union, not to have any part of it. She is now the chairman of the health and safety committee. So there are changes happening in that direction, although we still have to think hard to find them. The seed is planted.

ANNE: A major concern right now is job creating, since so many people missed their stamps this year. We're trying to get a federal grant for some work this winter, and we're trying to start more long-term co-operative workplaces, owned and operated by the workers. Eventually these might provide some more jobs. 'Cause the plant's not going to last forever. It's going to be closed one of these years. It's a marginal plant as far as Nickerson's is concerned.

I'd like to see co-operatives and alternative employment get off the ground here to the point where the women are controlling more of their own working lives. Mind you, that's not what the women themselves are consciously concerned about. They want jobs. Making some kind of income. Some of the immediate health and safety concerns, like slipping on the floors, and broken wooden steps. Arbitrary discipline will get them, but only when something's current.

My hope is that the co-op will answer both needs. It will be centred on their main concern, which is just having a job of some sort, and breaking the loneliness and isolation of the winters where there's nothing for them to do but sit around at the kitchen table and drink. And from my point of view, it will be a better vehicle for political education than the union ever was. Where women could talk about their lives and their work. Over the machinery at Lizmore, nothing important ever comes up. There isn't the time. There isn't the energy.

So on one level I'm hoping that we can replace the plant eventually with something better. Meantime I'm fighting for this union. You know you're trying to create some kind of unity in it. You're trying to develop some leadership. You end up fighting like mad for the union and being labelled as a union type for it. It's ironic, because the union isn't even where I want to be. The union is so contradictory, you end up policing the women in the plant. You end up fighting the union leadership on the one hand and the company on the other. You end up dealing with sexism on both sides. You end up trying to politic within the union to get it to back you up so you can fight in the plant. I mean, unions have been tame in this country. You end up fighting for something that you feel ambiguous about yourself.

GINA: What was your term for Lawrence, a "crumbs-off-the-table unionist"?

ANNE: Yeah. That's what I called him after one meeting, because he's constantly saying, "The company's having hard times right now. We must leave them alone. We must support the company because when the company's doing well, we'll be doing well." If they're having a bigger meal at the table, more crumbs will fall off the side for those of us waiting below.

There's a part of me that wants to stay involved with the union, to start politicking, getting more militant people involved in the Seafood and Allied Workers to pick up the banner and march out of the CLC [Canadian Labour Congress] and into the CCU [Confederation of Canadian Unions] which represents Canadian workers better. (Laughs.) Or take our local and march out of the Seafood and Allied Workers into the Fishermen's Seafood and Allied Workers, or take the whole Canadian Seafood and Allied workers and go join the more militant Newfoundland union.

So, on the one hand, I'd like to see us get out of the union business altogether, to create alternatives like co-ops. It's the same thing I felt in the church. I'm a born-again pagan now. (Laughs.) My feminism pulled me straight out of the church.

GINA: But it gave you a lot of good connections. Several times it saved your neck.

ANNE: That's right. The resources I had from my church work have been valuable. Everything from printing to finding a lawyer. But my experience with the church was the same. As you radicalize, you are tempted to take the group you are working with and go out and form something completely new. It's the same question about whether you'll be an independent local or join another union. On the other hand, in the long run it might be more powerful if you work inside and become the leavening for the whole institution and radicalize it. It would affect so many more people's lives. But is it realistic to think you can?

I was one of those urban, middle-class radicals, working with groups for whom all this was a hobby. I had trained as a deaconess with the United Church, where good church people have this hobby of social justice. And it's like finally finding a group of people for whom these issues are life and death. I've got so much energy from it. I'm not dealing with people for whom it's "interesting." I went home this fall and saw the way my parents discuss this kind of issue. "You know," I said to my sister, "I could be crawling through the backwoods of Nova Scotia on my belly with an M-16 slung over my shoulder, fighting a violent revolution, and my parents would say, "That's very interesting. A little extreme. But very interesting." (Laughs.)

I took a trip last winter, to Nicaragua. And it was like having a direct shot of inspiration, straight to the vein, to see young idealists like us trying to build a new country. They really are; their basic concept is to take over control of their state, of their government, on a national basis, and build something new.

GINA: For me it's not that large. It starts and stops with Lizmore. But I'm not the educated person that Anne is. The gut issue for me is, generation after generation these women keep going into the plants. They bring their daughters in after them, *their* children go in after them. It goes on and on forever. The gut issue for me is hopefully to make these people aware of themselves as people first of all, and secondly to make them aware that they have rights, normal living privileges. You do *not* have to work in situations like that. You do *not* have to toe the line. You have the right to work in a clean, safe environment where you're not oppressed.

Working here's made me very much aware that there are people who don't live the way I do, that everybody's not the same. There's no such thing as equality. It's made me realize that you can't sit on the fence forever. You gotta jump off onto one side or another and make a commitment somewhere along the line, and live by it. You can't give up. Like, I no longer live there. The job is gone, but the commitment is not and it never will be. It's not going to stop here. I made a commitment to the working class everywhere, within myself. That's the change it's brought about in me. It's as simple as that.

The Lizmore Seafood Plant closed down in April 1982. David, the manager, was transferred to another plant in the Nickerson empire and was subsequently fired. Gina was working as an office clerk for a salvage yard at the time of this interview. She is currently working in a second-hand clothing store in New Glasgow, owned and operated by a co-operative of women. Anne has been involved in the creation of several winter work projects funded by federal grants, as well as in establishing several co-operative businesses, most of which are run by ex-Lizmore workers.

Coordinators *Penny Lane and Jamie Kass of Glebe and Centretown Daycare Centres, Ottawa, Ontario*

PLAY FAIR WITH DAYCARE

PENNY LANE
&
JAMIE KASS

I ARRIVED AT *Penny's daycare centre on a windy summer day, with sun and shadows chasing one another across the playground. Small kids were running everywhere, squealing, playing with each other and teasing the daycare workers. Penny rushed in, late from an appointment, then led a quick tour around the centre. When we went outside to photograph her, the kids mobbed her, hamming affectionately for the camera. She was quick, easy and comfortable with them.*

Penny and I walked the few blocks to Jamie's centre, where she was just finishing up for the day. She moved out to the tiny backyard playground with a sigh of relief. "I haven't been able to get out with the kids all day." She posed with the kids, and when she got up to leave they hung on to her, not wanting her to go.

At Jamie's house, we settled in with a large pot of tea.

JAMIE: I got out of university in 1974 with a B.A. in psychology, and a few months later I went to work at Centretown Daycare. At first I worked with the preschoolers, and then I opened up the kitchen. Until that time the centre had catered food, which came in little black boxes — no smells, except rotten ones, and very poor nutrition. So we got a provincial grant, opened the kitchen, and I started cooking for thirty-seven children.

About a year and a half ago I began co-ordinating the overall running of the centre. I handle the budget and payroll, deal with staff and their problems — but not from a supervisor's point of view. (Emphatically) I'm not management. I get accused of it once in a while. (Laughs.) I oversee what's happening in the rooms, make sure that things are flowing smoothly. I try to work with the children a little bit each day too, but that's not always possible.

I love it. We have children from six weeks to five years old, and I find the differences in the age groups fascinating. You can do a lot of creative things with the children. They're with you for ten hours a day, so you're always trying to find things that will stimulate them, at the same time caring for their basic needs.

After a while you get this need for a connection to the children. One weekend we went to a union convention — heavy politicking, heavy floor battles, running around, lots of knives in the back. It had been a really exhausting, totally draining convention. And I came back on Monday morning and it was a nice day and all the children were outside. And it was like, *this* is the real world. It not only matters, but it's a lot nicer world.

PENNY: I'm a co-ordinator now too, at the daycare where I work. I'm in the office away from the children, which I have some regrets about. I really miss them.

At first I planned to be a teacher. I finished teachers' college in Toronto and then moved to Ottawa. I couldn't get a teacher's job so ended up substituting in the school system. My sister was working in the daycare where I am now, and I started substituting there too. I much preferred working at the daycare, but I felt I should teach. The more time I spent at the centre, though, the more obvious it became that that's where I wanted to be.

The schools are so formal and structured. The barriers there between you and the children are absolute, especially as a substitute. It's like being a warden at a prison. And the teachers were only concerned with things I didn't think were very important. They always talked about children in terms of their problems, why you wouldn't want this child in your grade next year. The parents were afraid of the teachers. They had power over their children's lives.

I found the atmosphere at daycare generally better. In daycare it was considered important to develop a good relationship with the parents. They were much more apt to create an equal relationship. And I just really liked the children. So a job came up in the toddler room and I took it. I was working for a lot less than teaching but it was so much more enjoyable.

I wasn't sold on daycare before. I even had some of those fears about institutionalizing children, taking them away from their parents too early. But the more I worked in daycare, the more I realized they really enjoyed it, it was good for them. They were being stimulated and well cared for. They were getting a lot of love, and their parents were able to go out and work and be happy, and not be nervous all day about what was happening to their kids. So, working there I developed a real respect for daycare.

JAMIE: Most people don't have it as a priority to put their child in daycare. They say that a private babysitter could be just as good. But one of the things you're working with in the field is how poor private arrangements can sometimes be. Women taking care of too many children, maybe ten at a time. Inadequate spaces with inadequate nutrition. Lots of TV. Those are the kinds of stories parents come to us with.

In group daycare you work one-to-one with the children certainly, but at times you want to give so much more to one child who you know needs it at that particular time. But you can't single out that individual child and neglect the needs of the group. So sometimes there's a real pull between what you want to do and what you know you can do. A realistic kind of pull. I don't think it's necessarily always negative, because the kids get so much socialization out of the process. They turn to each other and learn to help each other. Their socializing skills are incredible.

PENNY: We're constantly trying to reassure parents that daycare is a positive thing. You deal with parents' guilts. Most parents who come in are still the mothers, and they still have the most guilt because they think their "place is in the home." But once the parents start coming around and spending some time there, they begin to see how positive it is.

JAMIE: I work a lot with parents. Because it is a co-operative centre, we encourage parents to spend a lot of time there, to come in, have a coffee, sit and talk about their child or their problems. Also, you're there as a resource person, to let parents know what other resources there are in the community.

PENNY: I spend a lot of time with parents too. Sometimes I feel inadequate. I'm not a psychologist or a trained counsellor. But there aren't any counseling services for single parents, so they come and talk to us. Often I can do nothing but listen and offer a shoulder to cry on.

JAMIE: In the co-ops, at least in Ottawa, you have a philosophy about parents being involved and active on the board and on the various committees. The board of directors is made up of four parents and three staff members. So decisions about the operation of the centre are shared by parents and staff.

The staff are active in every aspect of the centre's operation: fund-raising, maintenance, the works. You feel that the centre is part of you. You care about everything that happens to it. In privately owned and municipal daycares there's a more hierarchical model, with the co-ordinator as boss, and different levels of pay. But in co-ops there's the philosophy that all the staff — cook, co-ordinator, teachers, janitor — are paid the same wage. Our funders give us different amounts for each job, but we equalize it.

PENNY: The work can be very stressful. Besides the physical exhaustion, you have a lot of responsibility. A lot of that is internal responsibility, especially at co-op daycares where there's nobody around to tell you to do something and make sure you do it. You're always judging yourself: you should have done this, you should have done that. You watch yourself. And the staff monitor each other.

One of our most difficult problems is the financial constraints, not being able to do what you want at your centre, not being able to buy new equipment, have a better building. Our centre is in a basement. It shouldn't be there. Look what we build buildings for! The Bank of Canada building in Ottawa. Daycare centres cost a miniscule amount of that.

But worse than that is that parents are being denied access to daycare, either because of lack of space, or because costs have gone up and they don't qualify for subsidy. We have ninety children on our preschool waiting list. People are calling just desperate, crying on the phone, coming into the office, hoping that with a little personal contact we'll let them in.

JAMIE: Being a co-ordinator has made it that much more intense because you hear it every day, hear the parents telephoning and *needing* space. Not needing it two months down the road, but tomorrow. I had a woman call today with two kids, a fifteen month old and a three year old. And she needed space within a month or she'd have to go back on mother's allowance. Her grandmother had been taking care of the children and just couldn't do it any more.

PENNY: And then you go from that to having to stand in front of a politician who tells you there's no need for daycare!

One of the hard things about our struggle has been that increasing our wages has resulted in a cost increase to parents. You see parents having to take their child out of daycare, out of this place where they're happy and well cared for. I find that really hard.

Most women we see *have* to work. But because our costs are escalating, because subsidies are being cut off, daycare is becoming too expensive for many parents. For a preschooler now it's $350 a month; for toddler and infant care, $500 to $600. Poorer parents can get subsidies to pay the whole shot.

JAMIE: That's the bind. Many parents who want to put their children in daycare just can't afford it. You're cutting off the whole spectrum of middle-income parents.

PENNY: Women can't ever attain equality working until they have good daycare. It just isn't going to happen. And whether it's right or wrong that daycare's a "women's issue," when it comes to the crunch, it tends to be. Sure, more men are taking responsibility, having custody, but women still have the lion's share, and if they can't find good daycare — not just during the day but for meetings at night, for union conventions, all of that — they don't have the same opportunity. Until that responsibility is shared equally, they're tied down. Because the children are so important. You can't just write them off.

But daycare as it stand now represents women's inequality in the workforce. And for the workers it represents the whole underpaid young working women's ghetto. One of the problems with daycare is it's mostly women. We're presenting children with a skewed picture of the world. There aren't many male daycare workers. And that's wrong. So you can hit on a lot of women's issues within daycare. But unfortunately we go back and forth: is daycare a woman's issue?

JAMIE: We keep saying no. But at the same time we know that women are the ones that are taking it on as an issue.

PENNY: If men had responsibility for children most of the time, daycare would be there. (Laughs.) It wouldn't be a question of building one more, we'd be building fifty more.

JAMIE: A steelworker had custody of his son and couldn't get daycare, and one of our trade union brothers was saying that *this* is why we have to fight for daycare! (Laughs.) Like it was so novel. This was an important issue: a man was denied a job because he couldn't get daycare.

PENNY: Daycare has always been poorly funded. Staff salaries were always kept low because otherwise the centre just couldn't float. A few years ago we were told that there would only be a five percent increase in daycare funding. Well, inflation was at the rate of eight or nine percent. It meant a cut in our wages. That was an impetus for us to do something. Not only for our own salaries but for the service. This year would be a cut in salaries, next year it's the whole centre going down the tubes.

So we called a meeting to discuss the funding situation. We dropped leaflets at all the daycare centres across the city calling for daycare workers to come out and look at the situation. About seventy-five people attended.

JAMIE: And that was unusual. It was one of the first times it had happened.

PENNY: At the meeting unionizing came up quite spontaneously. We had representatives from the city daycare workers, who were unionized within the large municipal workers' local CUPE 503. They were making $12,000 to $13,000 a year. Well, when I started, I was making $7,900 a year. My gross paycheque was $300 every two weeks for a long time.

JAMIE: We were the best paid co-op, and we were making $8,500.

PENNY: Somebody from a co-op got up at the meeting. "The difference between city workers and us? You're unionized and we're not." Someone else got up and said, "Obviously we should be looking at unionizing." At that meeting we struck a committee of representatives from ten daycare centres.

We were totally surprised. We hadn't called a meeting to unionize at all, but to discuss efforts to get public funding. The idea had been to form a daycare workers' lobby group to affect the political system. We had certainly discussed unionizing before, but it had sounded pretty vague and ominous. We didn't know much about it, so it hadn't come up as a clear option. But at the meeting it became a real alternative. We struck a committee to research the possibilities of unionizing. We had all these meetings...

JAMIE: We were diligent! (Laughs.)

PENNY: ... where we would ask each other questions: "Do we unionize? Is it feasible? Will we hurt daycare if we do?" We had to go through this soul-searching. Some people were afraid that we would sacrifice the welfare of daycare for our salaries, that we would jeopardize our relationship with the parents or our board of directors, because "everybody knows unions create havoc."

JAMIE: Fees would go up, per diems would go up, and could parents afford it anymore? It was ingrained in daycare workers that they should subsidize the service. They always knew it, but there was never any avenue to get out.

PENNY: We decided we were fed up with that, and also that in unionizing we might be doing something not just for ourselves but for daycare. That it needed to be done, that parents needed to be organized to get more daycare, that rather than helping the situation by continuing to subsidize it, we were just per-petuating it. If people were organizing just to get a bigger salary, they wouldn't be in daycare in the first place. It's the lowest paid job going.

JAMIE: And people had been leaving the field. You'd seen all your friends just leaving, even people who were politically involved in fighting for more daycare, seen them getting burned out in the struggle of trying to survive. And that left fewer and fewer resource people, and it brought new people in that were getting burned out at a greater speed.

PENNY: To be a single parent working in daycare had become just impossible. The only way to manage it would be if it were a second income, a not very necessary second income at that. Or to live with parents. Otherwise, it was pretty impossible to live alone on that salary.

It took about three meetings with a number of people to make the decision to go for a union. Some people had real reserva-tions, others were gung-ho from the beginning. We then had to decide how we could do it, and with whom? We asked people from different unions — from CUPE, from OPSEU and from SORWUC, which is the women's union on the west coast — to come in and speak to us about their union. We prepared a list of questions that we asked each union representative: What would you do for us? What do you think of daycare? What are your dues? What is your autonomy?

JAMIE: What's a collective agreement? What's a union shop? It was down to the most basic questions. Because we didn't know anything. But we were also testing them, because we were thinking of forming our own separate union.

PENNY: That was a thought. With SORWUC it would have meant pretty much forming our own union. They would provide moral support but were in no position to provide structural support. And that was a really attractive idea to a lot of us. But our obstacles were already so huge that we felt we needed a larger organization with resources to teach us, and we eventually decided to go with CUPE.

We went from centre to centre, with union cards, which went very quickly, at least in centres that had been involved up to that point. We immediately got eight centres, signed up pretty much all the people in every centre.

JAMIE: We tried to get more, but we knew that at some point we had to amalgamate with what we had. There was a lot of work to be done. We had to figure out how we wanted the whole local to be set up, so that everybody could have representation, and we had to begin to look at collective bargaining, which we knew very little about. So at some point we decided we'd take on what we had then, start the process, and once we had the process working we'd be able to go out and organize other centres.

PENNY: There were individuals within CUPE — Lofty MacMillan, Larry Katz — who were very helpful. Right away they understood the importance of daycare and proved subsequently that they weren't just talking but really did know our needs. I mean, in daycare you scrounge for everything: pencils, paper. But there were these people in CUPE who'd say, "We'll write a pamphlet for you," and they'd produce the pamphlet, or a sticker that said: "Play Fair with Daycare." It was a real high.

JAMIE: The workers were excited. It was new, it was something different. Some of them had reservations, but they were beginning to see it as a positive thing. It's what kept me in daycare for this long. I would have left it at least two years ago if it hadn't been for the union. It's such a positive experience. Sitting down and writing up a collective agreement — and we were the most picky bunch! They drew up a master agreement for us and we went through it clause by clause, saying, "Yeah, but what about this, and what about that? How will it affect the children? How will it affect the parents?"

Overtime. We'd never, ever received overtime. And so to think that we might, that we *should* be paid overtime! Even after unionizing it took some people two years to claim for overtime. And you had to push them to do it. It's really hard to get people to realize they have a right to the money.

PENNY: Part of the high we felt came from the friendships that evolved among daycare workers, just so solid and really caring. Friendships built on a different basis than before.

JAMIE: Penny and I are a union friendship here. (Laughs.)

PENNY: These friendships were based, not just on liking each other and sharing common views, but on this fight that you believe in. You were constantly reassuring each other. At the beginning we heard: "We've done this wrong thing. Daycare's going down the tubes, and it's all wrong and our fault." We were certainly warned of this by many people.

A lot of people in daycare are there because it's a nice thing for nice girls to do. To unionize is not nice at all. I think there's an old-guard reaction.

JAMIE: The old guard is people who've been around the daycare community for many, many years, and who always felt that day-care teachers were being underpaid but were never able to do anything about it. They have all those fears of unions. They were afraid that we would stop caring about the children and that we would only care about money.

Good example: breaks. You get a fifteen-minute break in the morning and in the afternoon. Sometimes we combine them in the morning because it best meets the program needs. They were afraid if we got that written in our contract, that if you were taking the children on a field trip, for example, you would *demand* your half-hour break. So therefore you wouldn't be able to go on any more trips. That's a legalistic way of looking at the collective agreement and how binding it was. Since we've been unionized, we've been able to show them that it doesn't change that way, and some of the things that do change should have changed a long time ago.

JAMIE: We always knew that there was a special problem union-izing co-operative daycare centres. We were told at one point that co-ops couldn't unionize because the parents and the staff sat together on the board of directors, that there was no clear management, and we'd never get certification. We ended up going for voluntary recognition: our parents voluntarily recog-nized us as a bargaining agent. So that let us over that barrier.

Then we had to start dealing with negotiations. We had a general meeting and brought it up before the parents. There was a fear of strike which we had to broach and deal with. But we also had to deal with how to bargain. So the parents had to be deemed "management," and one or two representatives from each of the boards had to come and sit at the negotiating table. We wanted joint negotiations for all the centres.

PENNY: Not all of them have agreed to join. The two profit-making centres were not involved in any joint negotiations at all. For them we had to prove it, go to certification, the whole legal route.

So we had one representative from the board of directors and one representative from the union of each centre, and we negotiated that way. The first year it took us forever to write up the contract, and then it took us forever to explain every clause.

JAMIE: Eighteen days sick leave. Some parents operated with only four to ten days sick leave. So we had to explain to them why we needed it.

PENNY: When you start working in a daycare, you go through this incredible period of catching every cold that goes by, let's not mention the other ailments you pick up. You get them all. And then you develop this rock hard immunity. But you sure go through it at first and you have to have good sick leave for that.

Seniority was an incredibly thorny issue for both the staff and the parents. A seniority system suggests to a lot of people a lack of merit — it's just any old person who's been there the longest. We had gone through such a learning process with trade unionists about what seniority means. It's a system where, if there's a promotion, or in our case a transfer, the person with the longest service who meets the qualifications gets the job automatically. And if for some reason management does not want to give that person the job, then they're going to have to say why, and the union has the right to grieve. It's a clear-cut method of promotion which rewards people for long-term service, and provides job security and new job opportunities for people who've been there. It's recognizing what people put into the workplace and don't necessarily get paid for. We were worried about, what if we have this feeling that they're just not the best person? We had to discuss this. Well, *whose* feelings? What *are* these feelings? If you've got a concrete reason, for example that the person is known to have a problem with that age group, then bring it up. Let's find out. Let's not just have these "feelings."

JAMIE: And in daycare it was so important, because a change in program or age of child that you're working with can provide a whole new interest. It can stimulate you, get you back to reading books and looking at things again. If you've been with one age group a while, you might really want a change.

So we put in a clause that in cases of promotion or transfer there would be a two-month probationary period. We told the parents that during that period they would have a right to say if it wasn't working out, giving clear reasons why it was not working out, and that they should at least give that person with seniority the right to try the job. And so far it's worked really well.

PENNY: It came home to me personally right in the middle of the contract negotiations. I'd applied for a job in a different room at the same time that somebody with more seniority had. I probably had a better relationship with the board of directors, and they would have promoted me. But because we were discussing it in negotiations, I withdrew the application. And this woman has done really well. To me it's been personal proof that seniority is right. It is absolutely right, because she had worked there for years and deserved the opportunity, and she's done so well. But that was something that we had no knowledge of beforehand.

JAMIE: What the union's done in the co-ops is brought a structure to them. It's brought an order of doing things that I now think the co-ops needed.

PENNY: You want to warn somebody? Make it a written warning. You want to have a disciplinary chat with them? Do it in front of someone. And then if you want to actually threaten somebody if they don't shape up, you can say, "I warned you here, here and here." Instead of just letting everything build up to a hysterical point: "This has been going on for a year!" "Why didn't you tell me?"

JAMIE: And one thing that never, or rarely, happens in co-ops is that you fire someone. But one fear about the union was that you wouldn't be able to fire anyone. Well, it wasn't done very much before we unionized, and it isn't done now either.

We have a clause stating that a worker who takes part in any political activity called for by the CLC (Canadian Labour Congress), its affiliates or subordinates, will not be disciplined. We're an affiliate of the CLC, so we could call a day of protest around daycare and we'd have the ability to go out without fearing discipline.

PENNY: But at the same time, we did that once, we closed the centres for half a day, but we didn't just walk out. We got substitutes — parents; we got buses for the parents. You only keep those clauses if you're responsible about them. We don't walk out and leave the kids.

We had this very thorny problem about what we were going to do about salaries. The money just wasn't there. What we aimed for was a catch-up with the municipal daycare workers. In order to make it more palatable we asked for a three-year catch-up, which *still* meant a forty percent increase for some workers in the first year, their salaries were that much lower. But we settled. We worked out all our salary schedules on a three-year catch-up — and this is very crucial — made the payment of those salaries dependent on government funding. Our strategy was that we would go *with* our boards of directors to the government and lobby for the money for our salaries. The contract would bind the board to carry this out. But if we didn't get the money, the centres were off the hook.

JAMIE: It was very unusual.

PENNY: We saw it as the only way to go. The private daycares agreed to go along too, and we're paying for it now.

JAMIE: They agreed to it, and now that the funding has come from the government, the owner of the two profit centres refuses to give the money to the workers. We're now going through grievances and arbitration and might be going out on strike with them because of it.

PENNY: With the others it went really well. We've had two years of catch-up now.

JAMIE: Centres are funded through the government, 50 percent federal, 30 percent provincial, 20 percent local or regional. In essence it became, who do you hit first: municipal or regional government? provincial government? And it's much more difficult for us to affect a provincial government than a municipal government. Just the location makes it more difficult. So we focussed on our regional politicians, and that's where we took the strategy. We lobbied two years in a row, large Play Fair with Daycare rallies at city hall. We drew up songs for the kids to sing, with a little political emphasis in them.

PENNY: We had placards to wave. And stickers made up. It was in August, nice weather, and we had people bring lunches, so it had that nice atmosphere. But it was still a political event. Both years, 1979 and 1980, we had about 350 parents, board members and workers come out to support us for those increased salaries. The argument to the councillors, even for those who had no use for daycare at all . . .

JAMIE: . . .or for unions . . .

PENNY: . . .was: "Listen, you're paying city workers $5,000, $6,000 more. We're employees doing the same job and you fund us both, so come up with it." They couldn't morally disagree with the argument, but they didn't like it because they didn't want to come up with the whole cost. They wanted to cost-share with the province. It wasn't easy.

I think that was one of the most exciting times, though. First of all, every victory was a shock. To win the first salary increases was just a terrific shock. The number of people who turned up for the rallies. . . .

JAMIE: We sat there holding hands and we were so nervous that it wasn't going to come off. And it was a two-and-a-half-hour debate at regional council before we knew that we'd won it. People were just coming up and saying, "We won! We won! We won! We got it!"

You see parents in so many different capacities. You see them as mothers and fathers, as people you counsel, as people with whom you work together lobbying for better daycare facilities and more money for daycare, as people you work with on community boards to make decisions about your own centres, and as people you face across the bargaining table. What does that do for you?

PENNY: It makes it clear that it's not us against them, the parents. It's us all together against the government. And we've developed a lot of respect for each other. I want a parent who's going to sit across the bargaining table to take it seriously. Because I find bargaining really hard. I have to say to myself, "I'm only here for the union. Stop thinking about the whole thing." I have to *only* think of that. And I want them to *only* think of the daycare. I want them to seriously bargain and only agree to things that will be okay. And sometimes that's hard, because of course you'll go out for a beer afterwards.

I think their natural sympathies are with you, and they would like you to have extra special leave for your own sick children. But they have to think, What will it do to the centre? Can we afford that? What if half our centre staff has children? What does this mean in terms of time off if you start adding it up? So they also have to wear two hats, and they have to see it from the board of directors' point of view. They have to look at it as management, but as fair management. I think they also have to look into it and perhaps say, "We can deal with that. We can swing that week, work it into the budget. That's a right."

People in daycare, of all people, should realize that consideration should be given to workers when their children are sick. We're always calling parents. Some of them have their jobs threatened when they're called to come and pick up their child because she's sick. They hate being called at work.

JAMIE: And as co-ordinators it's sometimes very difficult. We're the ones who are drawing up budgets. So at times you feel that you *must* give the parents a cost analysis of some of the union demands. Because they don't have an everyday working relationship with the centre. What you see happening is that parents are getting more involved in the centres. And I think that a lot of them are taking the responsibility very seriously.

PENNY: With the profit centres it's very different. Management has a lawyer who we negotiate with. It's very much more antagonistic, and especially now that the owner has reneged on her signed agreement. The staff there feel differently. They are angry. They'll go on strike if that's what it's going to take. However, even they are aligned with the parents. They've gone to the parents and said, "Look, she signed this agreement to give us this. We want you to help."

JAMIE: "You came down to city hall to that rally to help . . ."

PENNY: " . . .because you thought the staff were going to be paid more. But no, it's profits for her." And the parents recognize this. They know who's done the work at the centre.

JAMIE: We've gotten a lot of respect for what we've done, which has been much more than just negotiate salary increases. We've worked on the Day Nurseries Act, for example. We sat on a committee with a lot of different groups and worked to improve that legislation. Also, city council was trying to put a priority system into Ottawa-Carlton for parents, priorizing parents' need for daycare. And we spoke there at council meetings against it. We've lobbied for a ceiling for fee-paying parents. Right now we're getting involved in an idea whereby non-profit daycares would receive a direct grant from the province to bring down parents' fees, so that parents would be able to afford the service.

So the respect is there from a lot of different groups that used to look at us with that paternalistic attitude that people have towards young women who are getting involved, you know? Well, they're not looking at us with such paternalism anymore.

First we were just daycare workers, and then we were organized and negotiating a contract. Then Penny and I got out into the bigger world of a national CUPE convention. It was a fascinating experience. It was a really exciting convention. We were mind-boggled. We didn't understand everything that was going on.

It's huge. It's held in a convention centre or hotel. Lots of men, so it can be quite threatening. Lots of drinking going on. (Laughs.) And there is a chair at the front, and people from different locals submit different resolutions, and those resolutions are gone over one by one. It's tedious at times. You sit there and you fight and you get upset and think, How could they have voted that way? You get all involved.

At the end of it, Penny and I just hugged each other and said,
"Hey, we're trade unionists." That was a turning point for both
of us, coming out of that first trade union convention. We saw
things with a much broader perspective than we had before.

Then the CLC convention in 1980. Three thousand people, all
the different unions. It was much more than just CUPE. And
daycare was coming up, and I'd say, "Penny, I'm not going up."
"Yes you are." "No, I'm not." "Yes you are. Get up there and
speak on daycare." Penny had much more experience in speaking by this time, and I'm scared to death of it. But I got up with
my little notes written out, and you had to stand on a box with
the mike. I stood up there and my voice remained solid, but my
hands started to shake, and then my legs started to shake, and
my whole body literally went into convulsions. Penny was standing behind me for support and I just kept on. I almost fell off
the platform. Penny put her arm on me just as security to make
sure I'd get through. I did get through it. And it's been a little bit
easier after that. I still tend to shake. (Laughs.)

PENNY: But what happened was people saw it. Like, this was no
prepared speech. These weren't flippant remarks. This *really*
came from the guts. And people were really *with* her. They
listened, and at the CLC people rarely listen. They were listening and wanting her to get through, and at the end — "Good
work. Glad you got through."

JAMIE: Women are very supportive of other women there.
That's something you really see in the union movement.

PENNY: Through the union movement we've met a lot of different workers, from old-age homes, nursing homes. A common-
ality I find is that people really care about their jobs. The
biggest beef of people working in nursing homes is cutbacks on
care, on the patients. If they somehow allied with the patients'
families, who are being ripped off in those profit-making nursing homes . . . I'm sure the families of those patients would be
shocked to hear the kind of wages they make. If they could ally
on that, the care would have to get better.

We always thought we were the worst off, but we've heard
some horror stories about other people's working conditions,
such as health and safety problems, which isn't something we

have to worry about, or sexual harassment — again we don't have to worry about that. An awareness of those larger issues has been a really important gain.

JAMIE: And links with other workers. An ability to make those links. Through the trade union movement you can connect with so many different types of workers in so many different kinds of working situations that you begin to get a much larger overview of what workers' strengths can be. You see that if you organize properly and keep talking and developing, you can have some control. Not always (laughs), but sometimes. Supporting each other, that's important. When we were fighting for our salaries it felt so good to see not only the parents out there, but hospital workers too, people from other social service agencies.

PENNY: And then during the hospital workers' strike we had fifteen or twenty daycare workers on picket lines at different times.

JAMIE: Without a union we wouldn't have seen it.

PENNY: We would not only *not* have gone on the picket line, but we probably would have been opposed to the strike. But all of a sudden we were seeing that person's struggle in our own terms. We knew the people personally and we just came.

On the other hand, women's issues tend to have low priority within unions, at conventions. We had one just this week. Women's issues were last on the agenda. Sexual harassment, daycare, equal pay, technological change, occupational health and safety, especially as they affect women. The discussion was too brief, it was at the end, and we lost a quorum.

JAMIE: People called for the vote while there were still people at the mikes waiting to speak.

PENNY: You see unions all the time with ninety-five percent female memberships and a male president.

JAMIE: You have to get women to understand that they can have those skills, that they *do* have the skills and should start using them. And sometimes the only way to do that is to put them into a position where they have to use them.

PENNY: It's an incredibly hard thing to do. But it's also exciting.

You develop more self-confidence, not just in public speaking, but in talking to a smaller group of people, being able to convince them. You get a feeling that you can win, a confidence in being able to win.

Jamie is still co-ordinator of the Centretown Daycare Centre in Ottawa and is active in CUPE. Penny has joined the staff of the Public Service Alliance of Canada, as a union service representative.

*P*ostal Worker Marion Pollock
Vancouver Post Office,
Vancouver, B.C.

SORTING
THE MAIL

MARION POLLOCK

I MET MARION in March of 1981, while yet another round of national contract negotiations was underway between the Post Office and the Canadian Union of Postal Workers. The union demand for twenty weeks paid maternity leave was a central issue in the negotiations. Women's groups and unions all over the country were watching to see how it was settled. Would CUPW stand firm? Was maternity leave a serious demand or a negotiating tactic, to be dropped when wages were brought to the table?

It was a real demand and it was won. Several other unions have followed suit. Gains like this have to be credited to the hard work of women like Marion.

I SORT LETTERS AND FLATS, which are magazines or brown manila envelopes, and parcels. I do three kinds of sortations. The first is the breakdown into zones in the Vancouver area. The second is breaking down my work area, which is North Vancouver, into letter carrier walks. And the third kind, which I do rarely, is take bundles of magazines that come in and hurl them to the proper zone.

I take a piece of mail, I look at the address, and I put it into the appropriate pigeonhole. I'm sitting beside other people and in front of a case which is broken down into maybe fifty small holdouts, and each one is for a specific postal zone. Sometimes I sort and forward mail for a specific town in B.C., or a major town or city or province in Canada. I look at the piece of mail, I say, "Mm, goes to zone 5," and I put it in the holdout for zone 5. I have a handful of mail in my hand and I just take it one by one.

I started working at the post office after I graduated from university. I didn't have a lot of self-confidence, and I didn't think I could get a job in my field, which was sociology. I thought I'd have to get an unskilled job, so I applied to the post office.

I had never worked at straight jobs before. I'd always done grant-type or student-type jobs. So the post office was fairly amazing to me. I had never done work which was as dehumanizing and as boring, and to which my presence or absence as a person made no difference. At the post office, what was important was that my body was there. I was really shocked. I didn't know places like that existed.

I was really shy, but I related fairly well. What I found really interesting was how these people related to me when they discovered I had a university education. They thought I was smarter than them. And it really took me a long time to sort of convince them that no, it's not because I was smarter that I went to university but because I had certain breaks and I came from a home where my parents could afford it.

I was put into the work area where there were the most union people. I was put there because they wanted to break up that group. At that time I was very sloppy and pretty overweight and they thought I was retarded or very slow. So they put me in with this group of union people particularly because they didn't expect them to have any influence on me. (Laughs.)

I hated my job. I thought it was boring, it was stupid. I mean, here I was, just sort of shoving this mail into this little hole, and it just — went somewhere.

It wasn't possible to quit. I was virtually unskilled, except for my unsaleable academic skills. I also didn't have the confidence to go out and look for another job.

I remember the first week, looking around. I knew vaguely this was a union place, though I didn't have any real concept of a union. But we began talking, and I found it interesting and exciting. I started going to union meetings very soon, although at first I just sat back and never said anything. The union made me feel that I wasn't totally powerless. It gave me a way to say "Look!" to people, to act on some of the things I hated most and gain some control. And I felt that I was getting some sort of connectedness, a sense of being part of something, which all through university and high school I had never felt. This wasn't an abstract feeling but in fact was developed through concrete things which could be seen.

The people I was working with pressured me to become a steward. The union was always really short of stewards. I had known one of the union people vaguely from school, so that was a connection. I was looking for a place to get active, and I had a lot of time to devote to the evening meetings and to doing work. I also had academic skills,which means that I could read a collective agreement with some sense of understanding. And I sort of felt good about my skills, which a lot of people coming in didn't. They didn't feel they could become a steward, because they couldn't read or write very well, which in fact is really bullshit, but that's how they felt. I really wanted to do something. I didn't want to work here or there and not have any control, any power. I wanted to be able to get back at management. And I thought that if I hated my job so much, that being involved in something like this would give me a broader overview. So I became a steward.

My first big union issue was stools. When we sort letters we sit on stools. There was always an acute shortage of stools. People used to carry them around with them and hide them when they went for breaks. It caused a lot of tension between workers. A couple of months after I started, an open fight broke out over the issue, so we started a big stools campaign. Within three days we put in 190 individual grievances, one by one. Management complained that this was a form of harassment. (Laughs.)

The next big thing I got into was racism. We had a supervisor who consistently refused to talk to these two Chinese women. And when she went up to the washroom to do can raids, she would always pick on them. We go to the washroom in our "unauthorized" break: people go there to take a break from sorting, to relax, unwind and have a cigarette. So supervisors regularly come up and do a can raid — they kick you all out. If you get caught too much or spend too long in the washroom, they'll discipline you. And this supervisor would consistently pick on these two Chinese women. So we presented management with a really well documented case of racial discrimination.

I was really naïve. I thought we had it really well documented; we had witnesses. I thought it was a case based on the strength and the righteousness of our argument. So I was really shocked when they denied everything and said, "It's a personality clash. She's not racially discriminating; these people are just over-sensitive." It was really an eye-opener. I thought, Aha! It's more than a question of knowing your facts and getting them together; it's a question of power.

Another interesting case I was involved in had to do with bereavement leave. This woman's father died the day before Christmas. Bereavement leave means you can have four days off, but they have to be calendar days. So she had Christmas, Boxing Day and two days after that. But they generally don't bury people during the holiday, so on the fifth day, the woman applied for bereavement leave to go to her father's funeral. They denied it. It was incredible. We grieved it and won.

I've been involved in counsellings and disciplines, people being caught reading, people being caught out of the building, people talking back when supervisors have given them orders, a lot of cases where supervisors have been picking on certain individuals, cases concerning health and safety — almost everything.

Management seems to have a penchant for picking on the weakest people and harassing them. The post office management reminds me of a fiefdom: each supervisor tries to build up their empire, and there's a lot of rivalry between supervisors. So in order to maintain their power, they pick on people.

Part of it is the kind of supervisors they hire, or used to hire: a lot of ex-army people. I think a lot of them are petty people, but also their power is petty, because in fact the only authority they have is the power to recommend discipline; they don't have the power to actually suspend anybody. So most of what they do is just very petty: being unfair, harassing workers, can raids, denying people overtime, not training people properly, personality clashes, which the supervisors seem to go out of their way to provoke and continue.

For the past two or three years they've been "counselling" people for non-attendance. I've been involved in a lot of those cases. Counselling is a disciplinary interview, where management goes in and essentially berates you. It can result in a letter on your file or a suspension. It really affects women. A lot of women take time off because they have kids or because they do two jobs, at work and at home.

I got my own first major counselling about two months ago, for reading the mail, a newspaper. They can only prove that I was reading for one minute — no more, no less. So I got a disciplinary interview, which took forty-five minutes. And the grievance hearing about it took another twenty minutes. So they're spending sixty-five minutes disciplining me for an offence which I allegedly committed for one minute.

A big problem at the post office generally, and especially for women, is favouritism. Supervisors send people down to work areas on a non-rotational basis, just move them around depending on whether they like or dislike them. Prettier women will be assigned to the jobs they like best. Supervisors won't assign women at all to certain jobs. Right now I've got to the point where I sort of do the male jobs, only because they want to have one token woman doing them.

There are a lot more women in the post office now than there were in 1974 when I started. Then it was primarily men, mostly Caucasian. Now it's mostly women, a lot of Chinese and Filipino women.

The post office hired Chinese men and women in the early

seventies at the beginning of the mechanization program
because they thought they would be more passive and wouldn't
be so active in the union. I think they also thought of Orientals
as more manually dextrous than non-Orientals, which they saw
as important for the advent of the automation program in Vancouver. It's created a real change in the social milieu. There is a
fair degree of interaction among the Chinese and the non-
Chinese, but because most of the Chinese are first-generation
immigrants, their first language is Cantonese, and they tend to
spend a lot of time talking among themselves. It's easier, they're
talking in a familiar tongue. Some of the white workers, both the
younger and older ones, are fairly racist — they don't like people talking in Chinese. But the changes in working conditions
and atmosphere have mostly been brought about by the switch
to automation, not by the advent of Chinese workers.

Automation was brought in by the post office totally arbi-
trarily, totally unilaterally. There was virtually no consultation
with the union. They brought it in with no understanding of
how it would affect people, how it would affect our jobs. It was
done on a piecemeal basis to "improve productivity" and to
weaken the union. In response, the union started a "Boycott the
Postal Code" campaign to protest the heavy-handed and unilat-
eral way that management brought in automation.

Our working conditions have changed in a whole bunch of
ways since automation. One is the influx of women. Right now
you'll find most of the women are concentrated in the Coding
and Mech (mechanization) area, which is the automated area. I
work in City Floor primarily, where we sort mail destined for
Vancouver, Burnaby, Richmond, New Westminster and North
Vancouver. We used to work according to a knowledge sort,
which means having to know that Alberta Street goes into Station J. Now they've brought in a simplified alphabetic sort, so
Alberta Street just goes to A, which is a real deskilling of our
jobs.

The job is a lot more fragmented too. As a manual sorter I
generally sort the rejects from Coding and Mech. We end up
getting the worst mail. So you have less involvement in how the
mail goes through. You're just involved in one very small process.

It's also a lot more noisy, in fact incredibly noisier, and there's much more of a factory-like atmosphere rather than a civil service type atmosphere now.

My work as a steward has also really changed over the past couple of years. Initially I spent maybe an hour a week doing union stuff. Now it's considerably more, probably two hours a day on the average. That's mostly because I became chief shop steward, which is an executive position in the union and means I had responsibility for three shifts in one section. Now I'm the grievance officer, which means that I also go to a lot of meetings with management.

We have a whole variety of different types of grievances. If you have a complaint, you write it up, what happened, and the steward processes it. We submit it to management, and a hearing is held with the labour relations officer, another representative of management, a steward and/or the person concerned present. A grievance is essentially the legal framework through which workers can uphold their rights within the collective agreement. It's a fairly cumbersome process, and more and more I'm seeing it as a process management uses to cool us off. At the time they put in a grievance, people are really hot. But about eighty percent of grievances — all except disciplinary grievances — go to the national level. Before the last contract negotiations, we had well over 5,000 grievances waiting to be heard at the national level. Once it leaves the local level, it's like it's disappeared into oblivion, just because of the incredible time gap. So it cools people out. It makes people think that they have recourse, which they do, and that they will win if something unjust has happened to them, which they probably won't.

The grievance procedure is supposed to be unbiased, but it's essentially stacked in favour of management. They have the control of the procedure, they set it up. You are going in against the person you're grieving against, the supervisor. Well, management is going to back up their members. They're not going to support a unionist. And regardless of how just your case is, they're not prepared to move from their stance. It's a question, particularly in the post office, of not losing face, of maintaining this image.

I see my function as steward as not only defending people but also spending time talking to them about various issues: the contract, shift scheduling, management harassment. I try to make these things public, so people will know about them.

It depends on the issue, but a lot of times I wander around from table to table in the cafeteria on one of our breaks. You can't do it officially because you have no right, under the collective agreement, but I think that is one of the most important functions of a steward.

As a woman I find it's a lot harder for me to be heard and listened to, and I've really had to fight incredibly, and often obnoxiously, to be heard.

I notice even now, when I'm sort of one of the leading people in the union, that I'll say something, and a man will say the same thing later and he's the person who'll get the credit for it. It really pisses me off. Even when I have expertise in a specific area, people will not listen to me, they'll listen to the man, regardless of the fact that he's a new steward and doesn't know what he's talking about.

I also have to deal with real sexist jokes and comments. A lot of people don't make those in front of me anymore because they don't want me to give them shit. But it's really been hard; I've had to really fight. And it's also been frightening in terms of what I've done to myself. Because in order to survive in that process I've had to adopt a lot of really male ways of operating. I've had to be very aggressive, be really loud and pushy. A lot of women are discouraged from participating in the union, because you can't operate as a woman. I've seen women in my local who've been really good, who wanted to be active, but who have operated in traditionally female ways and they've just been smashed.

Women stewards have a hard time getting recognized by management too. I find that when I go in as chief steward or grievance officer, and I go in with a man, they'll talk to the man. Most of the supervisors are men, and they'll look at the man, they'll direct their comments and questions to him and not to the woman.

We deal with the same thing in our own stewards' body. Out of seventy-five stewards, about twenty are women — that's with over half the post office workers women. When I go in to management with a male steward, regardless of who's done the work on the case, the man assumes he's going to do the arguing and I'm just there for backup, rather than discussing it beforehand and deciding, "Okay, you know more about this" or "You should get experience." We have to work to get our male stewards to make it clear to management that when we go in together we're equals, and they have to recognize us as equals.

The first women's issue that came up for our local happened at the end of an afternoon shift. It was a purse snatching.

The union local president at that time was a sort of gut militant but real jocko type, and when I and a number of other women approached him about the issue he said, "Oh, go to Marion, because you're just jealous, you want to be raped too," and things like that. And I thought, Arggh. We organized this meeting, which I guess was the first time we got women together on a local basis. We had Rape Relief there to talk about how we could protect ourselves going to and from work. But I was struck by the inadequacy of their suggestions, things like "Leave work at different times every night." Well, if you're on a shift, you get paid to one o'clock, and you can't very well leave at twelve-thirty. The post office is not going to let you. In fact they were not too amenable to our suggestion of allowing us to go around and try to arrange car pooling.

We've had women's issues for years, though they haven't been recognized as such. For instance, part-time issues are really women's issues, because most of the part-timers have always been women.

Part-timers first came into the post office in 1956. We have a lot of older women who have been part-timers since then. Part-timers were brought in as casuals to decrease the strength of the full-timers and to be used as cheap labour, so there's still a lot of animosity toward them.

We have to improve the situation for part-timers, because right now they're being shafted. It wasn't until 1978 that they even got the same increment as full-timers. They still don't have a lot of our benefits. It hasn't been fought as a women's issue, and I think we have to begin seeing it that way and fighting it that way.

Nationally, our union has been in the forefront of unions in terms of educating and working with members and trying to lead militant unionism. Well, a lot of that hasn't extended towards women at all. The only time they've done it is when they've been pushed. At the 1977 national convention, a number of people tried to get a resolution passed which had to do with organizing women into women's committees and bringing up educational issues relating to women, and they were smashed. And it was a lot of the women from the other locals who smashed them.

There's a reluctance to admit we have special needs. I sort of feel that reluctance in myself, and the only thing that saves me is that I am a feminist. Women at convention feel they've made it. They don't want to be reminded of their vulnerability. I'm really glad there's a women's movement to protect me from the possibilities of what I can do to myself by blaming other women.

Sexual harassment is a problem on all three shifts. On graveyard, where we have a lot of new members on probation for six months, it's really hard. Probation is set by the Public Service Employment Act, and we can't negotiate it, so you virtually have no rights. The people on probation are virtual postal slaves. And if they raise shit, there's a real possibility that they'll be released from probation: the post office doesn't have to give a valid reason for firing them. So the male supervisors really take advantage of that and harass the women, from "touching" them on their bottoms to asking them out for dates, or giving out women's phone numbers to other male clerks who've asked.

We have a lot of areas where just men work, and there's a sort of male camaraderie in those areas. So a woman walking by has to put up with disgusting comments all the time.

Then there's the postcards that come in from Hawaii, the kind with pictures of nearly nude women on them. These are passed around and a lot of jokes and comments made. The same thing when *Playboy* comes in.

Mostly the problem is verbal, but we've had a couple of instances where it's got into pushing and shoving matches where women really felt threatened for their physical safety. It's an increasing problem, not because it's new, but because people are just beginning to recognize it and feel comfortable talking about it. It's always happened, and the probation people have always been the most vulnerable.

Locally we've done a fair amount about it. We've put articles in our local's newspaper on sexual harassment. I wrote the first article. The day after the paper came out, every person on the floor had read the article. They saw "sexual" in the title and thought it might be interesting. And if I had never had sexual harassment before, after I wrote that article I heard every sort of comment and joke that was possible. I felt like going home and crying. It was just one of my worst days ever at work.

When I was chief steward on graveyard shift we showed a videotape on sexual harassment during one of our coffee breaks. It didn't spark a lot of discussion, but at least the women could identify that there was a problem, that it wasn't only them. They sort of felt if it's on videotape it's real, it has much more authority. But we haven't had any grievances on sexual harassment at all. People have gone to management and complained about it, but management refuses to take any action. They see the men doing it as sort of crazies. And in some cases the men have not been the most stable, so management won't recognize that it occurs everywhere. It's really hard for women to talk about that kind of stuff. It takes a lot of self-confidence.

At one point we got the president and secretary-treasurer to go down and give a worker shit, and sometimes the women stewards have also gone over and talked to a worker. But we wouldn't grieve against a fellow worker, ever. You can't do it, legally.

Eight months ago I went to a regional wage and contract conference to which our local had submitted a demand to have a clause put in about sexual harassment, and it got defeated. People argued, "How can you prove touching?" And, "Does this mean that if I look at you in the wrong way you get to grieve against me?" "How can you prove leering?"

And at national convention last July we drafted a policy statement about sexual harassment, but, unfortunately, due to the bureaucratic entanglements that happen at national convention, it never came to the floor.

One of the demands we're going for in our present round of contract negotiations is twenty weeks' paid maternity leave. We have a lot of Chinese women, and for them the question of having a family is really important. They want to have a family, want to have kids. We have a lot of women going on maternity leave, and right now that means you not only lose your pay, but when you go back you have to pay double superannuation for the time you were away, and superannuation is seventy-something a month. It's virtually penalizing women for getting pregnant and having kids.

In the last round of negotiations, one of the reasons we rejected the conciliator's report was because he didn't talk about paid maternity leave. The union leadership will follow it up, because they're becoming increasingly aware of the power of women in the union, and they don't want to antagonize that power.

One of the things we've been complaining about ever since I started in the post office, which was almost seven years ago, is sanitary napkin dispensers. Talk about campaigns — we had a giant campaign to get sanitary napkin dispensers installed in the post office. A giant campaign! (Laughs.) We put in grievances, drew up mass petitions, met with management, who were incredibly embarrassed and did not want to discuss the issue. They said they were personal hygiene items and we should carry them around in our purse. The next thing you know, you'll have to carry toilet paper around in your purse. But that was management's stock response. Some people, I don't know who, sent used sanitary napkins through the mail to certain members of management. So we got the dispensers in, right?

But we found it's been a really hollow victory. We wanted sanitary napkin machines and tampon dispensers, but we only have sanitary napkin machines; worse still, they don't maintain them. We have machines in most of the women's washrooms, but they've been out of order since 1978. Just recently, maybe six months ago, they got a new one, and they put it in the Coding and Mech supervisor's office. So if you needed a sanitary napkin you had to go into the supervisor's office, which of course no woman wants to do. It's just really humiliating. So the steward there argued to get it out. So they said, okay, we'll get it out. But it either stays here or it goes up into the cafeteria, or you don't get it. So as a result we don't have any workable sanitary napkin dispensers in the post office. Not one works. Not a one.

Generally there needs to be recognition that there are, in fact, women workers in the post office. For example, washrooms. All but one of the women's washrooms have urinals in them. They did not build the post office with women workers in mind. The issue is simply to be recognized as women.

I went to my first national convention this year. The Vancouver and Atlantic regions submitted resolutions on women's issues, and the second evening we had a special meeting on the needs of women in the post office and in the union. It was really great. And one thing I was so proud of: every male delegate from my local attended, which means that a lot of the work we had done had really paid off. At a convention a lot of drinking and stuff goes on, and yet these guys all made the decision to come.

This great woman from Labrador got up and spoke about how the national union had not fought very hard for the demand of paid maternity leave — we've had this demand since ad infinitum — and talked about how the representation of women in various locals did not relate to representation at national convention. And then people were getting up and talking about the problems of women both in the union and in the post office; making it really clear that the national executive board has a responsibility to start dealing with women. The women sort of collectively served notice on the post office that we are no longer going to be treated as second-class workers. Just incredible. For me it was the highlight of the convention.

I've been through three strikes now: 1975, which was a forty-two-day strike; 1976, a one-day strike in Vancouver around tech change; then 1978 was the illegal strike. I've also been involved in three separate sit-ins. I found the strikes really incredible. They gave me a sense of morale. I mean, in 1975 we were out for forty-two days, and we were getting stronger by the end. This woman in my sub who was very, very shy, very scared, approached me when she found out that she had to picket. She was too scared to picket; she wanted to stay and do things in the picket room. I talked her into picketing, and she came up to me after and said, "I'm going to reject this contract." And I thought how really amazing it was to see people come out during the strike, how we sort of gain a whole new layer of leadership and a whole new layer of activists that we never knew before. And to see the winning of solidarity within our union, to see the power we had; that we had strength and could in fact work together, fractious and fragmented as we were, that we were sort of unified. And working together. Everyone understood and everyone had a lot more respect and a lot more sympathy for each other.

'Seventy-eight was entirely different, though. We had a fairly low strike vote in Vancouver to go out, sixty to seventy percent out of a not very high turnout. We went out, and then two days later we were sent back to work by the government. And later we had a vote to defy the back-to-work legislation. We had a higher turnout, and a higher vote to defy.

What amazes me about strikes is seeing people I think of as sort of wimps — people who aren't prepared to defend or stand up for themselves — I see them standing up and fighting for themselves. That's really exciting. They really understand who is the union and who is the boss. We had to go back to work in '78 because of the threats of the employer and the refusal of support by the CLC. People were crying, not only the activists but the membership, because they had a real stake in it. But to me the most exciting part was just people standing up, and standing up together, and understanding, having a sense of their power, and saying that we can do it, and growing as individuals. Picketing is really boring; walking around the post office is not fun. But if you're doing it with twenty people, you can discuss a lot of really good issues, and it is a lot of fun.

I've learned a lot, working in the union, but mostly I've developed in terms of self-confidence. When I first came to the post office I had no self-confidence whatsoever. I was very, very shy. I wouldn't speak up, I wouldn't fight. I've gained an incredible amount of self-confidence, and I feel much better about myself; I feel that I can do things. I'm able to approach people and talk to them, which I could never do before, ever; it just killed me. Right now I'm a lot better at fighting for other people than I am for me, but I'm improving, slowly. I also feel a strong sense of connectedness. I really feel that yes, I am in the labour movement. I am in the Canadian Labour Congress, and even though I disagree with their orientation, I am a member, and what happens in Saint John, New Brunswick, affects me.

Things are really changing in the post office. Without a doubt, service is deteriorating. There's no question about it. There's no question that it's despite what the union wants. You've not had an adequate training program in Vancouver for years. New clerks come onto the floor, they're set in front of a case, given a sheet and told, "Sort." That's their orientation. If you had people who were trained sorters, there would be fewer missorts.

The fact is that the automation program, while it's effective in some ways, is not without kinks. The machines are not the smoothest running machines. The other thing is management's methods. We have a real big problem with staffing. About five years ago we had 210 people on city day shift; now we have 130. We've lost well over 300 people in the past three years because of the automation program. But the automation program has not absorbed that mail; the mail has just been left around. You walk into the post office on most days and you see coffins and cages full of mail waiting to be sorted. They don't have enough trained staff to sort the mail.

Then there's the morale problem. Management is so petty, so pig-headed, that morale is terrible. Happy workers are good workers. The post office talks about the sanctity of the mail, but right now people are paying for first-class service and getting third-class service. You pay different rates for first-class and for third-class parcels, but the first-class parcels are being dumped down the third-class chutes. So people are paying higher rates and getting no service.

The simplified, ABC sort means the mail has to be handled a lot more now. They're shipping the mail out to smaller post offices to sort. This is their new way of trying to reduce both staff and militancy in the larger centres. The mail just makes a circle trip and goes back to Vancouver. Despite the fact that more depots have opened in the past ten years with the expanded population of Vancouver, the number of wicket clerks has decreased.

Security. They talk about security, saying we steal the mail. Well, the security in the registration system is so lax that you can open the door to the vault with a piece of string. Management does not follow the mail through. I've spent almost my whole day sorting third-class mail, and then they give you the first-class

mail to sort. Foreign mail they leave to the very last. When they
can't find any other terrible mail for you to sort, they'll bring up
the foreign mail.

I see as one of my priorities for the future just being able to
survive in there, being able to go in there and put in eight hours
every day. That's getting increasingly hard. Jobs are getting
increasingly boring, more deskilled. Management is becoming
increasingly rigid.

In terms of the union, we have to work really hard to increase
the participation of women. We have to learn how to speak to
the needs of women members, because we're not doing it satis-
factorily now. The labour movement has to have programs and
policies that deal with the needs of women, rather than trying to
contain us, which is what I think the policy is now.

The other thing is we have to continue to build the union
overall, because we can end up being smashed. That really
involves getting women active. And making sure that we get
decent collective agreements. Because the survival of the union,
especially with the transition to crown corporation and with the
advent of electronic mail, is really threatened.

They are going to try and contract our jobs out not only to
electronic mail people but also to smaller post offices. That's
what's happening right now. Work and services have been contracted out to smaller posts, like drug stores, who hire women at
half the rate we're getting.

We're being smashed on the one hand and contracted out on
the other. And that's why one of my goals in the next few years is
to ensure we still have a union.

The only thing that would make working at the post office
good, because it's just such a mess, is if it were controlled by the
people who work there. Other steps can make it a better place to
work, but I think that until we curb management's use of arbitrary authority, the pellmell way they're bringing in change and
things like that, it won't be a good place. We'll have to have a
veto power on technological change, rigorous health and safety
standards, supervisors that are accountable to some sort of body;
a real recognition that workers are people, that we have to be
treated with respect and just not shat upon and seen as arms
who sort the mail or key letters rather than people with real

feelings; a recognition of the work we do as valid; a recognition of the older people and their special needs and their limitations; a real discipline procedure, a procedure in which you're inno- cent before proven guilty, rather than guilty until innocent. Just a recognition of us as human beings.

Marion continues to work in the post office and to play an active role in CUPW.

*T*elephone operators Shan Williams and Debbie Sherwood at
the B.C. Telephone Company,
North Vancouver, British Columbia

"B.C. Tel, Under Workers' Control"

S H A N   W I L L I A M S
&
D E B B I E   S H E R W O O D

I FLEW INTO VANCOUVER *during the lockout of the Telecommunication Workers' Union by the B.C. Telephone Company. The friend who was supposed to meet me at the airport wasn't there, so I went searching for a pay phone to call her.*

None of the phones worked. I tried phone after phone, losing a few quarters in the process, and becoming increasingly frustrated at being unable to reach my friend.

Eventually she arrived and pointed out that my anger at being inconvenienced was justified, but that it needed to be directed at the real culprit, B.C. Tel. Later, she arranged a meeting with two of the telephone workers who had just returned to work, but who had been active, enthusiastic unionists in the struggle to wrest a decent living out of B.C. Tel.

Though only twenty-six at the time of the interview, Shan was a veteran telephone operator and unionist. Debbie, at twenty-one, was new to both.

They quickly pointed out that the image people have of telephone operators lined up along a board with blinking lights and manual plug-in connections is no longer accurate. All that disappeared with computerization.

S HAN: I started in 1972, right out of school. It was the only job I could get at that time. I really enjoyed it, stayed for two and a half years. I took a year off and went away, but I came back because I liked the hours, the people I worked with, and I liked flexible days off.

I was a supervisor. I did all the initial training and review. You matched the volume of people sitting on the boards to the volume of calls that were coming through, you gave time off, made up schedules, sat on the board if it was really busy, talked to the customers that the operators couldn't handle or chose not to, or customers who sometimes phoned in and said, "Give me the supervisor." A little bit of PR with it as well. It was a good job, a lot of variety. And now there isn't any.

They decided they were going to change the whole structure. When they went into more automated equipment, into computers, they did away with the job that I did. Actually, it did away with management jobs, and the managers have taken *our* jobs. Now they've got this computer gadgetry which does all of their forecasting, says how many people they'll need on a given day. AMOS's (Assistant Managers of Operating Services) have taken over the work supervisors used to do, and most of us are back on the board.

DEBBIE: I haven't been there long, only since '79. When I started I really enjoyed it because it was something new, and I was just out of school. I guess it took about two months before I started getting frustrated and angry with the way it was being run. But I was living on my own and I couldn't afford to just quit. Plus I was going to school nights.

We were so supervised! They watch your ACV, average time per call . . .

SHAN: . . . how long it takes to get rid of a customer.

DEBBIE: They usually want that to be about thirty seconds. So if your average at the end of a day turns out to be about forty-two, you've done really bad!

The supervisor monitors these calls. You don't know when they're monitoring you. They do what's called an SP23 on you, which is a form they fill out once a year that evaluates everything you've done.

SHAN: It says things like: "How does the employee get on with other employees?" "Do you feel that the employee is mature enough to advance to a highly skilled job?" Both your work and your attendance are evaluated, and they mark you below standard if you've missed, say, eight days in a year. They give you a slap on the wrist and tell you that they're going to do it again in three months. Also you're constantly being indexed, which is somebody listening in from a remote position, making sure you're giving out correct numbers. The computer times all of your calls. If you get an ACV that's lower than the office average, which they set at thirty-two but really want to be thirty, they say, "You're doing it too fast. You're being too quick with your customers." If it's above that, they're telling you to speed up. "Get rid of them quicker than that. You're being too helpful."

DEBBIE: You're never doing the right thing. I've been told that I've been too friendly with my customers, too helpful in trying to find something, and then the next month told I was too businesslike; I wasn't spending enough time with them. So really, I don't think there's any time you can get a perfect record. There's always something that's going to be wrong with it.

SHAN: And if you do, nothing is said. You're lucky if they even show it to you. I don't know of anybody who's been taken off and told, "You're doing a good job."

I haven't had an index for about six months now I guess. And

I'm so unbusinesslike with the customers. But I get rid of them fast enough, and they seem quite happy. If somebody is treating me like a human being, I will respond like a human being. I am not part of that equipment. Twice I've been taken off the board on a Sunday by a first level manager who has nothing to do with me. She just happened to be in the office. She was doing what she calls "spot monitoring" on the terminal, plugging in and listening to a few calls from everybody in the room, just to make sure that everything was going okay. Once she took me off, because I cut off a customer. She told me I wasn't allowed to cut him off, I should hand him up to her. I said, "You don't take any of the calls I hand up to you anyway. So if I can't handle it, I'm going to cut him off. He was very obnoxious and he deserved it." That went on a nice little piece of paper called a prep sheet. I asked to see the sheet, and there were other things written on it that I had no idea were there, from six and eight months before. One wasn't a complaint. My immediate boss had taken me off the board when I was thinking of going to school, and we had a chat about that. She just wrote that down. And there was another comment in there that I had been seen filing my nails.

The other time she took me off the board, she accused me of telling a customer, as she put it, to "F.O." What really happened was that I had put the customer on hold and said something to relieve myself of all this frustration I was feeling. I went back on the line and told her that I couldn't help her and would put her over to someone who could. So this AMOS told me she was writing it up and was going to leave it for the second level manager to take disciplinary action against me. I told her if she did that, she would have one hell of a fight on her hands. It was an invasion of my privacy. What I do between calls, or when my customer is on hold, is my business.

The prep sheets are written up between evaluations, supposedly to help the managers write up your report. They're supposed to be destroyed after your SP has been done, but in a lot of cases they haven't been. We've had quite a few meetings about that.

DEBBIE: I've never seen my prep sheet, but I'm sure there are things written on it. I've been spoken to on a few occasions. One time I'd gone to work feeling sick. When I first started, I would feel very guilty if I called in sick, because every day after they would phone me to see when I would be in. They wouldn't wait for me to call them. That made me feel very bad. So this one day I went in, groggy. I had to take some antibiotics. I was really slow on my calls and had to have people keep repeating themselves because my ears were all plugged. And finally they came over and asked me just what in hell I was doing, because I was yelling. I couldn't hear myself. And I was told that I had no right coming in in that condition, that I shouldn't have been there, that I would pass it on to other people. They had badgered me to come in and now they were badgering me to go home. I'm sure that was written up.

Other times they've come up and talked to me about having magazines on the board. Not that I was reading them, but they sit with my purse or my lunch or whatever. They'll come up and actually take them away from me or tell me to put them under my desk or move them so my hands can't get at them. High school.

If you've had a good day, your office has a good average, they'll bring around candies or a box of cookies. They've got a blackboard where they write your average. If it's good, they'll write underneath: "Good work girls!" and underline it. If it's bad . . .

SHAN: The thing I find most disgusting is when they write up on the board: "North Vancouver — 30, New Westminster — 34, Vancouver — 36. Good work, girls. We're beating them!"

DEBBIE: I think if they took this time limit off our calls they'd probably get more from us. Nobody wants to work when they're being humiliated. You don't want to give anything to anybody.

When you go to the washroom you have to put up a flag before you go, and when you come back you put the flag down. It's like a tag system. If someone's already there, you have to wait. You can wait an hour. You have to find out who's in the washroom and count down. It may be ten people. If it's a real emergency, you have to go to the AMOS and say, "I'm going to the washroom."

SHAN: You kind of develop a negative attitude when you're being spoken to about how many times you've been to the bath-

room or how you sit at your position. I would take away all of
those rules and leave it up to the operators. If the operators are
mad because somebody's in the bathroom nine or ten times a
day, they will say something. You don't need any schoolteacher
breathing down your neck. Just relax all of that rubbish. If that
person is not doing the job, fire them. But if they are doing their
job, leave them alone.

DEBBIE: For the majority of people who work with Traffic, who
work as operators or in directory assistance, it's their first time
working. So they get in that department and think that's the way
it works. Until they've been in other departments or in a union
somewhere else, they don't know it can be any different.

SHAN: The only thing I knew about unions when I started at
B.C. Tel was that you don't cross picket lines. I never went to any
meetings or anything like that. I generally worked afternoons.
There didn't appear to me to be any conflicts at the time. There
were also no union reps around to sort of do the sales pitch for
it. I got involved after the lockout in 1978 and when they
brought in this new mechanized system, called "Daisy" (Directory Assistance Information Services).

The first weekend our office opened in North Vancouver, the
business agent from the union and one of the union counsellors
came over to hand out some meeting notices. So when they came
in I made some comment like, "Gee, I guess with no reps over
here, the big shits have to come out and do all this work, eh?"
And one of them said, "Yeah. Why? Are you interested?" And I
said, "Yeah, I am." And they called me every night for four
nights until the night of the meeting, to try to talk me into
getting involved. I would say, "Well, I don't know anything. I
haven't even read the collective agreement." And when I went to
the meeting, I went in not knowing what a union counsellor was
and came out a counsellor.

It's like a second-level shop steward. A shop steward would
deal with grievances, with the first-level manager. If they don't
get any satisfaction, it would come to me. And I would deal with
the second level and the third level. And if we still don't get an
answer that we agree with, I'll hand it over to my business agent
and she'll take it to Industrial Relations (Board). So basically

you're a sounding board for everybody's little bitch and gripe in the office. Quite often we've had quite a few grievances. Very seldom have we settled them at second level.

They're so petty. My first case was about a guy they refused to pay when he was attending his grandfather's funeral, because the grandfather was not considered part of his immediate family. He had to go to Squamish for the funeral and he was not going to miss it. The manager said, "Oh, that's really too bad. Maybe you can get the day covered." He did not go into work that day. He took the time off, and the company gave him a little slap on the wrist. So I read my contract, and there was a clause that said an employee shall be granted time off with pay for such personal reasons as wedding of self, relative or friend, or death of friends. So that covered his grandfather. But that had to go to third-level management before he got his pay.

Another time this girl had come into work one day and worked just about her entire shift. Coming up to hour six she's feeling really nauseous. She had a really bad headache all day, and she went up and asked if she could go home. They said, "We can't spare you to go home. But it's up to you. It will be on your record, though." She said, "Well, I was out in the boat all day yesterday and I must have got sunstroke. I'm really ill." She went home, missed the next day, and came back into work the following day. She was informed she wouldn't be paid because, they said, sunstroke is a "self-induced illness." We went into third level with that one, actually wound up in Industrial Relations. And the company still refuses to pay for sunstroke.

When we deal with management, the grievor is generally not there. If the grievor is there, that's counted as my witness. I have a witness, management has a witness. It's better if the grievor's not there, really. You get everything written down on a piece of paper, exactly what the problem is, where it occurred, what occurred, what the collective agreement says about it, what the company has said to them. You get the grievor to sign it, and then they're out of it. You take it out of their hands. You go and deal with it. Because lots of times it just creates bad feelings between someone who's felt they've been dealt with unjustly and their immediate superior, say. It's not necessary.

For quite awhile I was the only union rep in the office. They will not give anybody time to talk to me at work, unless I'm on coffee and they're on coffee. If someone asks to see me, they say, "Do it on your own time." So I hear about most problems over the phone at night or in the morning of a day off. They phone and say, "I'm getting fired. Can you help me?" And if I go in, the company has said, "You're coming in on your own time." I say, "I'm quite aware of that." "Well, we're not going to pay you for it."

If they schedule a grievance meeting when it's my day off and I go in for it, they say they won't pay me for that either. You're supposed to get paid for time and travel to a grievance meeting.

Another thing that annoys me a lot is, I'll go up to a first level manager and say, "There appears to be a misunderstanding here. You were saying to this operator that you will not pay her if she goes to a wedding." And the manager says, "Why didn't that operator come to me? They don't have to go running to the union all the time!" And they go and start hammering on the operator about wanting this buddy-buddy system. But it just doesn't work that way. It can't work that way.

We haven't had a collective agreement in fourteen months. The company's been stalling negotiations, waiting to get rate increases from the CRTC (Canadian Radio-Television and Tele-communications Commission). Last September they locked out 530 of our people for "low productivity." They were on a slow-down. The union had told them to go in and only do emergency work. They work in Special Services, Construction, working on construction sites downtown that need boards put in, wiring, things like that.

Well, we decided that instead of calling rotating strikes we'd be a bit more organized this time. We'd hit the area that would do the most damage to the company but would still provide the majority of us with jobs. Those of us still working would sub-sidize those that were laid off and also put pressure on the company to get down to bargaining in good faith.

The laid-off workers were getting seventy percent of their wages, from people donating twenty-six dollars every payday. Then the company started to lock out in other areas of "low productivity," as they called it. We called it "superservice." (Laughs.) And it wound up in January at our convention that there were a thousand people that were locked out.

The CRTC gave B.C. Tel their rate increase on February 2. The company made another $47 million. But there was an interesting clause at the bottom of the CRTC agreement that said the company had to prove that service had improved by the fall or they'd take back this money. So everybody figured, that's great. They're going to have to sit down, give us an agreement, get our people back to work to get the service done. But what they did, which was just brilliant, was to turn around on the Tuesday, February 3, and lock out another thirty people in Nanaimo. So Nanaimo took over their buildings.

We'd talked about this tactic at the convention. We'd debated it for about a day, and it had been agreed that it was only to be used as a last resort. We weren't going to go out there on Monday and take over the building. It was only to be done if the time came when everything broke down and there was no other recourse. And we felt that after the CRTC gave them their increase and they turned around and started locking out more of our people, it had come to the time.

We discovered during the last lockout that they made half a million dollars a day every day we were out. And that they kept us out until they felt they'd made enough money.

DEBBIE: They were charging for service during this time, and the public is still paying for it . . .

SHAN: . . . while B.C. Tel was paying a third of the people they normally would have. The reason we wanted to take over the buildings was to guarantee we'd have jobs to go to. We wanted somebody on the door to let us come in. Because if we started doing rotating strikes, they'd lock the doors and that would be it. We'd be out, we wouldn't have any PR behind us, any support. They'd be raking in three-quarters of a million dollars now and we'd just be sunk. We don't have the numbers that we once had. We don't have any clout as far as threatening to walk off the job. Big deal. We walk off the job and they're making money and that's what they're there for.

On Thursday the fifth, just before lunch, I had a message to call this girl. I phoned and she said, "Call Russ at this number." Russ was the strike co-ordinator for North Vancouver. I phoned. He said, "Hi Shan. Today's the day." And I said, "Have you got twenty plant guys beside my door here?" "No." "You'd better get them here."

Pretty soon plant people start coming into my office. They were telling the second-level manager, who leaped up as soon as she saw them, that they'd come to have lunch with me, that they were just visiting. So by about two-thirty there were thirty of them there, just visiting. (Laughs.) And we were going around telling people that when they finished their shift, they were to remain in the building, we were taking it over. So they made arrangements to get babysitters, and husbands, all this kind of stuff. And it was going really, really well.

I was kind of scared at first. I wasn't sure we were going to be supported. I actually expected half my office to walk out. But that didn't happen. The strike co-ordinator got hold of me again, told me that my people shouldn't be working, that we were the only office in the province that was working, and that we had taken over the building and to be sure to tell management that.

So I went up to the manager and said, "I have to go and talk to someone. And, just for the record, we've taken over the buildings." (Laughs.) I walked out. As soon as I walked out the door, she went over and shut off the stereo, stood in the centre of the room and said, "I'm sorry to inform you that you are on strike now. Would you all please leave." Now the clerk comes up to me and says, "Shan, get in there. Elly's telling everybody to go, that we're on strike." So I go running in there. I was mad that she didn't do this when I was there, but as soon as my back was turned. So I said, "I think that's pretty sleazy, Elly. We're not on strike." "Yes you are. You've taken strike action. I am still the manager of this office. You shouldn't be talking to me like this." And I looked, and not one person in the room had moved. They'd all just unplugged and stayed sitting there. So I thought, Well, maybe we *are* going to make it.

I got on the phone to the co-ordinator and he said, "Nope, keep working. Finish off your shift. We're going to have to carry it on from here." The only problem was that our office closed at eleven-thirty at night, whereas the downtown office was open twenty-four hours. So about quarter to four I get a call from my business agent who tells me to take everybody out. And we all left the building.

We had a local meeting that night. I got home at nine-thirty and got a phone call at quarter past ten to get downtown to the Daisy office. They haven't taken over the downtown building yet. And *I* have to take it over.

Now, I don't know them and they don't know me, and I don't know their managers and *they* don't know me. It was really quite cute, though. There's about five of us, I guess, and we all walked in. Starting on the tenth floor we went up to the manager and said, "As of eleven-thirty tonight, your services will no longer be required. We're taking over the building, and you can go home, stay in your offices or whatever you want, but you're not doing any work." They said, "Do you realize that this is a strike?" We said, "Well, no, it's not a strike. We're guaranteeing our employees that they have work." She went around and told everybody that they wouldn't be paid and that they were on strike, that they should go home. We told everybody just to sit still. They didn't leave their positions.

The AMOS continued to work. She was answering all the phones. She was leaning on all the sheets and papers and schedules and stuff like that. So I went down to this other AMOS's console and I got the repairman to come by, and I said, "Look, they're not letting me do anything up here." And he said, "Okay, we'll just shut down that position."

He went downstairs and pulled a couple of switches and shut off their computers and opened up the one where I was sitting. So as soon as she realized what was going on, she got up and ran into the office to tell the other manager. And we ran up and took all the sheets, came down and started working. So we were there all night until the next day, and at ten o'clock in the morning just about the entire North Vancouver office showed up downtown to help out. 'Cause that office was locked, bolted. There was no way we could get into it at all.

We stayed in the downtown office for five days. Some of us slept there. We got to go home twice, for a shower and change of socks.

Management came in on Friday, stayed till about ten-thirty and then went home. They came back Saturday about seven for a couple of hours. They just left it to us on Sunday and Monday.

DEBBIE: I'd gone to night school Thursday and heard what had happened. So I went into the North Van plant, across the street from our business office, and someone said, "You know the girls in Daisy?" and I said, "Yeah." And he said, "Well, we want you to stay here the night." I said, "Okay. But I've got to go and get a sleeping bag."

I didn't think I could do it. I didn't know a lot of the people. I'd never been active in the union, and I didn't know how they would feel about somebody that sort of sat back in the office, never really got involved, telling them what to do. As it worked out, we ended up with everyone downtown.

So I went downtown and walked in and couldn't believe what I saw. All these people from my office were running everything. The positions were full. Work was going fine. People were talking. It was more relaxed. At the same time there was electricity. The vibes coming off people, the auras around them were just vibrant, unreal. The people I worked with had seemed so humdrum, and here they were _alive._ All of them were glowing! Because they were doing something they believed in.

SHAN: We talked about having a co-op tel, provincial ownership. The front of the building had signs saying: "TWU Tel," "Co-op Tel," "For Sale."

DEBBIE: We were answering directory calls with "The Embassy."

SHAN: Or, "TWU, under workers' control."

DEBBIE: Shan made a point of going around telling people what was going on so it wasn't like they were sitting there not knowing. They were told, or had an opportunity to ask. If they didn't believe in being there, then they had an opportunity to question it. You weren't locked in. You only had to put out what you thought you could afford.

SHAN: The North Van and the Burnaby offices were closed down. All of those calls were being directed downtown. And there was one other Daisy office in New Westminster, but it's only open until midnight. So then we had calls coming in from all over the province. All of the graveyard staff showed up. Every night. Some of them would even come back at six the next night and say, "Look, I'll be in the coffee room if you need me, 'cause I think it's going to be kind of busy tonight." And that was a real shot in the arm!

DEBBIE: There was one girl I got a phone call from. She was in Banff on her vacation. She had two weeks to go. She phoned me and said, "I just heard what happened. I'll be in tomorrow." And she was.

SHAN: Then on the Monday we got into training the plant men how to operate the Daisy equipment. It was kind of a horror show to begin with, but it turned out great.

DEBBIE: They had always taken for granted what we did. But for the first time they were sitting at the positions, getting the calls one right after the other, and they felt the uneasiness, the frustration and everything else that goes with that job. And they couldn't handle it. And yet there was no management breathing down their necks, timing them, doing all the things that we were fighting to get rid of.

SHAN: It was the best PR that we got. When we came out of the buildings on Tuesday, the Cable 10 people were still around. One of them said, "I've got something to tell you that will probably make you feel better. We were talking to this plant guy last night, and he said that he did your job for free in the last few days, but he wouldn't do it for fifty-five dollars a day." I says, "We don't get paid fifty-five dollars a day."

We had this big media tour on the Sunday. Everybody came in, all the radio stations. Cable 10 gave us really good coverage. Anybody who wanted to talk to them we made sure could come off and talk to them. It was just wonderful, getting our side of the story shown.

DEBBIE: I had an interview over the phone with the *Seattle Times*. (Laughs.) That was fun. The reporter just dialled 113 for B.C., came through and said, "Let me speak to whoever's sitting up front." So I got on the phone, said, "Hello, can I help you?" and so on.

SHAN: The thing that was so magical, though, and I'll never forget it, is the support we got. I made a point of sitting on the board whenever we were busy, 'cause other people knew how to run the office. And the public was so bloody good. It was like a big shot of adrenalin. They were punctuating each call with: "Stick to it. I hope you get what you're after." "We're behind you one hundred percent." "I hope the company gets taken over." It was like all of your relatives and loved ones were on the phone talking to you, you know?

DEBBIE: Even now, being back, it's really good. People phone and are yelling in your ear, "We were behind you all the way, but it's good to have you back." Every fifth call you get someone saying, "Welcome back."

What was happening during those five days?   Were any negotiations going on?

SHAN: No. (Laughs.) Nothing was going on. I think we were on our fourth mediator at that time. Talks had broken down. The company was just being its arrogant old self.

DEBBIE: They were just stalling for time.

SHAN: This time the main issue was the jurisdiction clause, which deals with contracting out. They can give away a large section of our work to a private contractor, for example buy cable from some company and have the company do the installation work. And it's just work — and money — coming right out of our area.

Also, this contract was the first time — since the Seventies, anyway — we haven't been held down by the Anti-Inflation Board. So we wanted to get decent wages and upgrade the wages for people like operators, to close the wage gap. We wanted two dollars an hour across the board. The company comes back and offers us seven percent for the year, total package.

The company wouldn't budge at all on the percentage increase. They'd made a decision to give us a percentage and that was all there was to it. They wouldn't even discuss anything to do with an hourly across-the-board rate.

In a percentage raise, if you're making $100 a day and get a 10 percent increase, you add $10 to your pay. If you're making

$50 a day and get a 10 percent increase, you only add $5 to your pay. The gap goes up from $50 a day to $55. The rich get richer and the poor stay there. (Laughs.) The purpose for the across-the-board raise is to close the gap, at least in percentage terms, to upgrade the jobs in operations where you don't get paid for the job that you're doing. It's very hard, very stressful at times. It was just ridiculous to have our wages held down the way that they were.

Also, the company was trying to eat away at our bargaining unit again. They had this one group of technicians, tradesmen, whose wages they would continuously upgrade, meanwhile keeping ours way down, by giving a percentage increase. A lot of these technicians figure they're management. I think the company is trying to make the technicians' jobs management jobs, and eventually that's probably what's going to happen. But it does erode the bargaining unit if you have a faction there that wants to break away. So it was just not a fair deal.

On the Monday, which would be the ninth, the courts came in with an injunction to get us out of the building. We had done a lot of thinking about what would happen if the injunction went through. I would like to believe I would have stayed if we'd decided to stay. But probably once the RCMP looked me square in the eye and said, "Get out of here," I would have got out. The courts gave the company the licence to lock us out, so that was it. The union said we would leave the building.

They gave us until noon the next day. People gathered all morning, and by noon there were about two thousand on the street from all the unions, CUPE and CUPW, a guy playing bag-pipes. Everybody went down to the basement and started walking out the door.

After that we were locked out for seven weeks. We picketed. Walking up and down the street on a picket line isn't a lot of fun. But when you think that because you're doing that you are eventually going to get a settlement, you can feel good about it. You can walk out of the building on Tuesday morning when you've got a court order telling you to get out or go to jail, and you can hold up your head and think, "Okay, we did it. We ran the company for five days. We showed 'em." (Laughs.) You do build a certain amount of confidence.

Some days you felt pretty good. You put up a picket line, and all these courier services and truck drivers would drive by with little words of encouragement. People with businesses would come out and abuse you, and you'd say, "It's okay. Don't get telephone work done and we won't put up a picket."

I had a nice job one day. I went around to all these banks with little letters, asking them not to accept B.C. Tel bills. Two of the banks weren't accepting them, but one was. Said it was a service they had to provide for their customers. They said, "But we're not going to take any sides in the matter." I said, "Well, that's fine, then you won't object if I put up a picket line." So I went and made a phone call and walked back to the bank and started marching back and forth.

It's a bit distressing at times when people you know cross the picket line. A relative of mine crossed my picket line.

DEBBIE: A girl I used to work with in Daisy crossed mine. We were picketing B.C. Hydro at the time. Some worker from Hydro phones us and said they'd put in a bunch of cables for B.C. Tel, so we put pickets up. She walked right up to me and said, "Hello," and I said, "Hi," and she said, "I'm crossing your picket line." (Laughs.) And she is one person who has been through a strike, who knows what it's like. That was very hard.

We picketed the ferries (to Vancouver Island). They had an agreement that they wouldn't help to transport any telephone vehicles or supervisors that were going to do any work, or let anybody service their coin telephones. And they stuck to it until management sneaked in to deal with a coin telephone. So the ferry workers phoned us and said, "You've got a guy in here." So we sent pickets out and held up the ferries for four hours. The ferry workers wouldn't cross the line. They went off the job. That was a hard picket line. There were lots of people who wanted to go home on the ferries. Some drunken man came up and started throwing pennies at one girl, which is frustrating because you don't want to aggravate the public.

SHAN: We had good success with our flying squads too. Everybody was paired off, always two people. Usually it was a woman and a man. As soon as a B.C. Tel truck went out, they'd follow it wherever the guy went. They'd walk in and talk to the people and tell them what was going on. One time we went down and followed them to a car dealership. The two supervisors went in, we got out our signs and walked in right behind them. The dealer was standing there talking to them, looks around, sees us and says to them, "Sorry, you're going to have to go."

DEBBIE: One woman at the plant Christmas party, a manager's wife, said that she was going to be really glad when we went out on strike because it would pay their mortgage and buy them a new car. The managers were being paid a special rate, plus dinner allowances, to cross the line. And most of the time, with the flying squads following them, they sat in their trucks or went and had coffee or sometimes even went to a bar. One guy had his picture taken sleeping in his truck.

SHAN: They had reached a tentative agreement about two weeks after we were out, but it was conditional on the CRTC giving the company another $47 million. So the mediator packed his bags and went back home. He said he hadn't come across that kind of third dimension bargaining in his life. He thought it was quite disgusting. We got another mediator a couple of weeks later. They reached another agreement, but they wouldn't allow us to come back to work with the twenty-five people they had fired during the lockout. Some of these people had charges pending. But the majority of them were fired for using obscene language towards a manager, or one guy was fired for throwing a bucket of manure at a supervisor that was crossing the picket line. This was after the occupations.

DEBBIE: One woman was fired because she had run into a management person in a Safeway grocery store and the manager threw a bleach bottle at her, so she kicked him.

SHAN: What we agreed to in the end was that a lawyer up in Prince George would review all the cases and make a recommendation that would be binding. So of the twenty-four, fourteen were allowed to come back to work with us and the other ten have to go through arbitration.

We had fourteen months with no agreement and another seven weeks out in the street. You gotta decide what's more important, having some money or fifty dollars a week in picket pay. We weren't going to get any further with it. Even the mediators all came in with recommendations for percentage increases. So we're kind of stuck with that.

I voted for the settlement, purely because I could see us being out for another two or three months and wind up only getting one more percent. I've got a lot of faith in our bargaining committee. I know the people on it. I think they did the best that they could for us. I think that if they were recommending acceptance, then they're the ones that know.

But I didn't like it much.

DEBBIE: I voted to go back too. I'm sort of sorry that it's over. I spent a lot of time down at the union office and got to know all the people there. And I got to know them in situations where there was a lot of anger, when there was a lot of relief, when they were really happy because we'd done something really well. I mean, you got to see these people in just about every emotional phase.

The union became people to me. I wasn't alone anymore. It wasn't just Traffic, it wasn't just women, it wasn't just management. It wasn't phoning over to the plant and not knowing who was on the other end. I'm sort of sad that I'm not going to be seeing these people on the same basis as we've been seeing each other. It was sort of neat today when I got off work to walk out of the office and see the plant guys and women coming out. "Hey, how are you?" Before that, you'd walk by them and wouldn't know who they were. You didn't care. But now you care. You want to know what it's like over there now that they're back. They want to know what it's like where we are. So it's a sad feeling in some ways.

SHAN: I'm not glad it's over. (Laughs.) Simply because I don't think that we got what we deserved out of it. It's not just money . . .

DEBBIE: I don't think it *is* over.

SHAN: Well, we're back at work, right? And they sent around trays of doughnuts for us on Monday, and candies. Downtown they put out flowers, but we just had doughnuts and candies. Probably came out of our coffee fund. (Laughs.) They weren't so sweet that the board was dripping with honey or anything like that.

The second-level manager looked at me first thing Monday morning and said, "Good morning." That was the only contact we had all day. I was really angry on Monday. I couldn't explain why, but I was really angry. I didn't want to have to deal with any kind of insincerity or bullshit. I don't agree that management didn't have a choice but to go to work, and I don't agree that because they had to work ten hours a day and they're tired that I should have some sort of humanistic feeling towards them. As far as I'm concerned, because they were in there working, I was out on the street. If they had come out for one day and had a study session, we would have had a contract. But they didn't offer us any support at all, so don't give me any lip service now.

I have kind of a conflict. I wonder why I continue to work in a situation like that, when maybe I could be off in something I'd be happier with. I don't like to see people taken advantage of. And that's all that company represents. And if I have anything to say about it, I'm going to say it. And if I have an opportunity to do that in the position I'm in, if I kind of stay there for that challenge ... But perhaps that energy isn't going to be a positive thing for me. I'm not really sure.

I just know that for as long as I work for this company, I'm definitely going to be involved in the union. Nobody's ever going to change my mind about that.

Shan and Debbie are still working at B.C. Tel and active in the Communication Workers' Union. Since the interview, Debbie has joined Shan as a shop steward.

Secretary Joan Meister, Library,
Simon Fraser University,
Burnaby, British Columbia

HARD BARGAINING

JOAN   MEISTER

I MET JOAN *in her bright, warm kitchen rich with the smell of fresh coffee. It seemed a long way from the negotiating table.*

She started working for Simon Fraser as a student in 1968: "Almost every semester break, about one month in four. I did very boring clerical stuff, alphabetizing and processing forms, doing coding for admissions. I have a capacity for doing stuff like that very quickly. I make games out of it to make it go faster. Which gave me a good reputation with supervisors. In one job I typed a lot of bibliographies and actually quite enjoyed it because I like typing. I love using IBM machines. (Laughs.) I do. I find them aesthetically pleasing.

"I actually ended up with an honours B.A. in Medieval Literature, knowing that I wasn't going to get a job using it. Still, I was *disappointed when I had to work as a secretary in the library. I reconciled myself to it. You're in the middle of lots of things happening. It's a good context to keep on with your learning if you feel like it. You can wear anything you like.*

"I was one of the original signing members for AUCE (Association of University and College Employees), Local 2, back in 1975. I'd always sort of believed in unions though it wasn't something I would make this big stand about."

I N JUNE 1978 I RECEIVED this funny phone call from the president of the union. He said, "I was given your name by someone who thought you might be interested in taking minutes for a contract committee meeting." Well, the only reason I know how to type is because I've done a lot of it. I don't have shorthand or those kind of skills. So I said, "Are you sure you've got the right person?" (Laughs.) And he said, "Yes, if this is Joan Meister." I said, "Well, surely to God in a bargaining unit of this composition (clerical and technical support staff) you'd be able to find someone who can do shorthand. I couldn't do minutes for you. Well, try to find someone else, and if you can't, phone me back." Sure enough, I got a call back from this fellow saying, "I didn't come up with anybody else." Everybody else said, "No. Are you crazy?" (Laughs.)

Somehow I was under the impression that I was going to take minutes for the one meeting. This woman who later turned out to be the union co-ordinator handed me a large binder, a stenographic notepad and two pens. I thought, "Gee, that's a lot of stuff for taking notes at one meeting," and off we went to "caucus." I didn't know what that meant. So we went to this room and I stated my piece: "Look, I don't know how to do this. I've never really done it before. You're going to have to take what you get. As long as you're prepared to go with that, I'll do it."

So then someone said, "Oh, you'll get used to it." I said, "What do you mean, I'll get used to it? This was going to be one meeting, wasn't it?" "Well, no. This is the contract committee and we're going to be negotiating with the university and it could take a few months." That was in June 1978. It wasn't settled until November 1979.

Our first negotiating session was very interesting. There were three of them from management, and at the beginning there were six of us. On the other side was this fellow named Chuck Buchanan, an ex-military type. He's got a crewcut and is quite jowly, and he's actually fairly chivalrous in a completely chauvinistic kind of way. ("Now, dear. . . .") But he was so obnoxious in that first meeting that I could hardly believe it. He set the tone from the very first day we met. His style was so antagonistic and oppositional, there was no notion of compromise or negotiation. He would start all his sentences with "Absolutely not. . . ." or "Under no circumstances. . . ." I developed a shorthand, "U.N.C." for "under no circumstances," because he used it so often. Or, "We won't move one inch, not one inch!" He said things that were patent lies, things like, "You're the best paid workers in Canada. . . in North America . . . in the world." We used to go, "Oh God, heaven help us. What's going on here? This guy is outrageous."

Chuck was, and still is, the head of ancillary services, which takes care of telephones and all the other services which the university needs to keep running smoothly. He's the head of traffic and security, and even of safety in science labs, which have radioactive material in them. Whew! He had been the negotiator for the first two contracts as well as this one. He had a definitely confrontational style, old-fashioned blood-and-guts kind of stuff, taking the gloves off, everybody getting bloodied, old-fashioned labour relations. Things have got quite a bit smoother lately. Things have gotten so smooth you can sometimes hardly tell one side from the other. But he was really of the old school.

In this environment it didn't take me long to radicalize. In about three sessions I was raving! (Laughs.) From the beginning there was a bone of contention about where the bargaining took place. We were bargaining in the administration building, in a room with no windows. And there was one member on our team who was very bothered by smoke and he wanted to have a room with windows. We tried to get the university to move us into a more central building on campus, and especially one that wasn't in *their* camp. I mean it was in *their* building. We didn't want to be there. It put us at a disadvantage right from the start. But we couldn't budge them out of that room.

At one point the other side brought in coffee and doughnuts. Well, we were so indignant by this time that we weren't having anything to do with their coffee and doughnuts. It was as though they were poison. "Nooo! Do you think we're going to have coffee with you and eat your rotten doughnuts? No!" (Laughs.) This actually set up an interesting dynamic, because they tried a couple of other times to bring in coffee and doughnuts and we simply refused. It acquired a fairly inflated importance after a while. Then they gave up.

We met in some kind of boardroom with a long set of tables that curve around and have an empty middle. And they used to sit over there (gestures) and we used to sit down here. Well, one day, it must have been about the second or third session, we ended up sitting at the other end of the table. Honest to God, I don't remember that we intentionally sat in their seats. We simply went in and sat down. When they came in they didn't even sit down. Chuck said to us, "Was this done with malice afore-thought?" We were sitting there going, "What's he talking about now?" and we sort of looked around. He said, "I'm leaving. When you're prepared to sit in your own seats, let me know, and I *may* come back." And they walked out.

What were we going to do? It was nuts, just nuts. We got to be quite seasoned in that respect fairly soon, because we were presented with one encounter after another that was totally beyond our experience.

One thing we used to talk about a lot. You know, you're brought up to be kind of polite and truthful. You don't make a point of lying and being rude. Most people don't. (Incredulously) But they did this all the time. We eventually decided that we were being far too principled with them, far too honest and too polite. The only way to fight this was to give them a little bit back in kind. But we never managed to do it very well, because we simply couldn't bring ourselves to be anywhere as rude and obnoxious and devious as they were.

It's a very interesting situation when you know that empirically you have a case. Inflation goes up eleven percent, so there's really nothing wrong with asking for an increase that would take into consideration inflation. That's not hard to figure out, is it? But they used to counter us with outrageous statements. I guess because they couldn't counter it with anything sensible. That's the kind of thing they usually accuse the union of doing — you know, those "boorish union types."

Well, it wasn't too long before the whole union bargaining team was made up of women. And this guy Chuck was facing a real dilemma because he was brought up to treat women in a chivalrous fashion. He would be the kind of man who would open doors for you. We got the sense — we talked about this a lot in our various caucuses — that he felt faced with this terrible problem when women whom he expected to act a certain way and expected to be able to treat a certain way, acted quite differently. I think we challenged his patriarchal notion of how things ought to go.

Once he got over the idea that he had to treat us like girls, like ladies, though, he was able to be as vicious, or even possibly more vicious, than he was with men. We weren't into backroom deals. We weren't into going to the bar after sessions and all being together and patting each other on the back and talking about what a shit-kicker of a session that was.

I gather that their whole style of negotiation is different when they negotiate with the poly-party unions who represent the trades workers on campus. Now, far be it for me to say that the poly-party unions suck up to management or anything like that. But it so happens that they're men, and they deal with each other on the level of male to male, right? They can swear at each other, for instance, 'cause they're just a bunch of boys. They can sit around calling each other cocksuckers and stuff like that. But while we would have liked to do that, there was something that held us back. I mean, I sound like a fishwife sometimes. I'm quite a garbage mouth. But we weren't able to talk like that in negotiations. We felt some kind of constraint.

Another thing that was especially demoralizing was that there was one member of their team who had previously been a member of our bargaining unit, and who had in fact been a

negotiator for our bargaining unit. And she had gotten a management job and was now sitting across the table from us. It was
very demoralizing. Mind you, it also gave us a focus for our hate.
(Laughs.) It was a deliberate choice on their part. For one thing,
she knew the contract much better than any of them! I even
used to feel sorry for her. What a horrible position to be in! She
doesn't have a contract to protect her. She couldn't tell them to
go fuck themselves. She simply had to be there. I don't think she
liked it much.

From a very personal sense of outrage I started feeling a very
special solidarity with the other members of our bargaining
committee. We had to work so hard and so closely together.
Originally there were six of us. Two were men, but they fell by
the wayside as things got harder and tougher. We actually asked
one man to leave because he seemed quite irresponsible and was
not prepared to take part in the collective decision-making process that we absolutely adhered to. The other got threatened
through work about his involvement on the contract committee,
and he just caved in and stepped down. A third man was
appointed, but he got a job somewhere else. Much later we
heard by-the-by that two other men were going to come in and
sort everything out, fix it all up for the girls. (Laughs.) Well, they
dropped off pretty quickly too.

So there were five of us, all women, and we developed this
incredible bond. When you're struggling with any kind of
oppression and you're doing it together with other people, you
develop those kinds of bonds. And that solidarity starts with the
women you're working with but goes beyond that, so that you
feel it with the membership as a whole. You feel, *we* are a group
of 650-odd people, and we deserve better. These are not unfair
demands. They're not outrageous. We're not doing anything
that's terribly off the wall. We're just trying to keep up with the
fucking cost of living!

It lasted such a long time, about fifteen months. Our contract
committee would meet every single Saturday. We would get
together at ten o'clock in the morning and we'd usually go 'til
about two or three, doing a lot of intensive, hard work. You're
not much good for the rest of the day, so you may as well call
that the whole day.

We were negotiating at the beginning about two days a week on the average. There we were. We'd sacrificed our Saturdays to get our game plan sorted out, to work on contract language and so on. Then we'd go to negotiations. It's not that it's such hard work, but it's emotionally draining, absolutely draining.

We would usually start negotiations bright and early in the morning and generally get out of there at maybe three o'clock. We would drag ourselves back to our not-too-exciting regular jobs knowing full well that those jerks on the other side of the table probably would take the rest of the day off, or didn't have much to do, being supervisors. (Laughs.) It was really demoralizing. You could see them leaving the campus in their cars. My desk was by a window that looked out on the main road. I could see them leaving and I would just get so angry!

We had a vested interest in these negotiations. The stakes were really high for us. We were representing 650 people, and that's a fairly big burden. As they drove off in their cars, I remember feeling, they don't have anything to lose by this! They're simply getting paid. They don't have any feelings. They don't have to go home and stay awake at night worrying: Oh God, how are we going to get this one? What are we going to do with that? How are we going to get the information to back up this demand? (Groans.) It's a long time ago, but I still get really riled about it.

It was demoralizing, but at the same time I was getting clearer and clearer about where I stood. I learned quickly who's us and who's them, and whose interests I'm working for and whose interests they're working for. I guess I developed a class consciousness: knowing which side of the fence you're on, you know? A class analysis came a little while later, but it definitely came. Knowing who was there with me.

Our union was founded on the principle of trying to achieve equal pay for work of equal value. And from the very first contract we fought for that principle. In the first contract we were quite successful, and we got close to it. It brought us to a kind of wage parity with some of the outside workers on campus. We made great money gains, thirty-odd percent increases in some cases, which brought us from dismally low wages to considerably better ones. The second contract was negotiated under the AIB

(Anti-Inflation Board) guidelines. We got 2.5 percent or something, which didn't improve our conditions particularly. Now, in
the third contract, we were once again going for the principle of
equal pay for work of equal value.

I'm not sure the principle found itself translating to the membership of the union. I mean, yes, the membership was in favour
of a decent percentage increase. But how many members are
actually aware of the principle involved I'm not sure. A lot of
people know what equal pay for equal work means. God knows
it's been ensconced in law for fifteen years, though not put into
practice. But when it comes to equal pay for work of equal value,
I think a lot of people are confused.

What it means is that I believe my skills, responsibility, duties
and working conditions should be paid equally to someone else's
similar skills, responsibilities, duties and working conditions. In
other words — this is one of our famous examples in AUCE —
the person who hands out library books over the counter, who
takes them, checks them against the cards and passes them back,
that person should not be paid $3.50 to $4.00 an hour less than
the man in the gym who accepts dirty towels and gives out clean
ones, right? Very similar working conditions. But the man is in
the Teamsters. God knows why. But there you have the difference between a man doing work and a woman doing essentially
the same kind of work, and a huge difference in the hourly
wage. When you point out that kind of example to the membership, people say, "Yeah, yeah." But I suspect that what's really
ringing bells is fifteen percent signs.

Because everybody knows about inflation; everybody knows
how hard it is to buy groceries on a wage that stays the same
while everything else goes up and up and up. It's very easy to
understand why we need a good increase. Now, whether equal
pay for work of equal value translates that need generally or
broadly, I really don't know. I suspect maybe not.

But because we haven't been able to get decent increases in the
last two contracts, the wages of the technicians have been low-
ered fairly significantly compared to the going market rate. And
though we brought up the wages of the clerical workers, they
still aren't great. So, inside Local 2 there is a certain antagonism
between the male technicians who are now below market and the

female clerical workers who are still struggling to get better wages. As a result of that, on our last contract we voted to take the increase we won and apply it in a percentage fashion, to try to catch up the men. It's a bad situation. The only thing that would fix it would be to get a really good whopping increase that would take care of everybody, that could decrease the difference between the wage scales but at the same time give everybody a boost.

So here we are, negotiating quite a large package of items, among them a fifteen percent wage increase. We met eleven times during the summer of 1978. The only things we agreed on were items like substituting a dollar sign for a cents sign because the computer couldn't accommodate the latter.

We weren't bargaining from a very strong position and they knew it. They didn't put their money offer on the table. They simply refused. They wanted to negotiate everything else and then do money. Which, as any dingbat can see, leaves you with absolutely no negotiating position when it comes time for money. There's no leeway. There's nothing that you can trade off or anything you can negotiate around because you've settled it all. But we weren't in a position to do very much about that, unfortunately. So we started off with all the easy stuff, all these non-substantive items like grammatical corrections, typos, adding small words here and there.

One of the most important aspects of these particular negotiations were the clauses affecting the temporary workers. We had fought very hard to get the temporary workers included in our bargaining unit. We were trying to get them better benefits. They don't get seniority, they don't get sick leave, they don't get hardly anything.

We had to dump the demands eventually because there wasn't enough strength in the bargaining unit. And because the temps were only here for nine hours a week, and because they tend to come and go as students do, I think people weren't aware of the more long-term effects of having a number of workers in our bargaining unit who simply didn't have the kind of benefits that the rest of us had.

That was a long struggle. The university is still trying to maintain that the temps are students first and workers second. The only thing they talk about in terms of temporary workers is the fact that they are students who are working there because they need the money, and the university is helping them out. Our position has always been and will continue to be that students are workers, and as workers they deserve the kinds of benefits that the rest of the workers on campus have.

Most of our student temps didn't scab. They did cross the picket lines as students. That was okay. They changed hats. They used to be workers, and since they didn't want to sacrifice the entire semester's worth of work, they turned into students and went to classes.

The other things we were going for were articles on reduction of the workforce and on contracting out. We wanted to have a clause that establishes that if there is a reduction in the workforce, there is a comparable reduction in the workload. Which means that they can't lay off or fire people and then expect others to take up the workload of the people who were dismissed. We didn't succeed.

The contracting-out clause says something fairly mild like: "The university shall not normally contract out work normally done by members of the contract unit." Well, the "normally's" give them a big loophole which makes the clause essentially useless. The clause didn't mean anything. We didn't get that, either.

We tried to beef up our medical and dental plan, the university covering a greater percentage of the costs. We did manage to get movement on that, but it wasn't particularly significant.

We were going for a COLA (cost of living allowance). (Laughs.) Didn't get that either. We were falling behind. Fuck, yeah, drastically behind. I mean we've lost something like twenty-two percent in the spending power of our wages over the last two contracts. With inflation piling up on the other side. Real wages are on the decline. Very much so.

So we started out going for fifteen percent and a one-year contract, not two. You don't want to tie yourself into a two-year deal, because you have no idea what the economy is going to do in the interim. You have no idea what kind of situation may arise in terms of working conditions that you would want to address over a two-year period. Some unions are accepting a three-year term these days. It's lunacy! It's craziness! It's simply not acceptable to tie yourself in for that long when God knows what else can happen.

Our contract had died the March before we started negotiating, in June 1978. We negotiated for more than a year without getting a money offer. So we applied for a mediator and got this guy Ed Simms in November 1979.

He was okay. He used to tell us these wonderful anecdotes about working in the brewery workers' union in Chicago, back in the old days. There used to be this big warehouse that had railway terminals coming in, and they used to lie down on the tracks to stop the trains. He told wonderful stories. He was a pretty good shit. That didn't mean he was on our side, no. I mean, he might have been on our side to the extent that since we were a bunch of women who obviously didn't know a whole lot about what we were doing, he took that kind of natural male protective, fatherly approach. But as far as what was going on at the table, he wasn't on our side any more than he was on their side.

Still, his being there made a fair bit of difference in that management couldn't allow themselves to be quite as rude to us. Also, at this point another member joined their team, the director of personnel services, who had a totally different style from Chuck's. Bill Yule. He was really smooth, smooth and slippery. And when Chuck started getting a little outrageous in front of the mediator, this guy actually kicked him under the table. (Laughs.) It was delightful. There was a sort of power struggle between the two of them. And Yule won because he was more senior and had obviously taken more up-to-date labour-management courses. In fact, eventually Chuck actually stopped coming.

In a way we missed him. You got accustomed to the obnoxiousness. And in a way, Chuck was sort of principled. His principles were *wrong,* but he was principled. So he was predictable. You knew what he was going to do. Yule, on the other hand, you could never pin him down. Sort of like pinning jello to a wall. You could never understand where he was coming from, except that he was patently on the other side. So we missed Chuck in a strange kind of way.

The mediator finally managed to get them to put a money offer on the table. They decided to offer us a four percent increase for a one-year period. And they were also going to give us a $200 bonus. Now, they had consistently tried to offer us bonuses in the past. And we had consistently refused, simply because bonuses are a lump sum that doesn't affect your base wage rate. Next time around, you end up negotiating from the same starting position. Which is why they consistently try to offer them. So we rejected the bonus.

At this point we took a strike vote. We were so inexperienced that we got to mediation without one. The mediator couldn't believe it. "What are you doing here without a strike vote? They're not going to have to pay any attention to you at all." So we took the vote. We lost. It's something we aren't very proud of. We just weren't in touch with the members. We only have one paid person, and that person has to do everything. And there wasn't a system set up whereby an information officer was pumping out information, making it very clear to the membership what all the issues were.

To make things worse, very early on when we didn't know very much about what we were doing, we made a verbal agreement with the university that we wouldn't do any kind of negotiating through the press. Well, (laughs) did we rue the day when we made that agreement! The fact is, we should have been going to the press almost constantly and keeping them informed about what kind of attitude the university had adopted, letting our membership know specifically, week by week, how things were going. Because when we finally got to the point of talking about taking a job action, the membership had no idea of what it had been like, how bad it really was. And to try and convey that a year after the fact, well, they probably didn't believe it. I just don't think they would believe that that whole kind of antagonistic confrontation was possible. You start to sound like a bunch of crybabies: "Oh, woo, woo, woo, we worked so hard and woo, woo, woo, they were so mean to us." (Laughs.) You sound like a bit of a wimp.

We realized a little too late that we should have been more in touch with the membership. It's not as though we didn't report at every membership meeting, but somehow it didn't get through. And we were so busy we simply didn't have the extra time. We were working to capacity. I think most of us were running flat out, on empty.

After we lost the strike vote we had to drop a lot of our package: eleven items. We were about to sign a memorandum of agreement, when the members rejected it on the basis of this four percent wage offer. So then we had another strike vote, successfully this time. That was in November. But unfortunately we didn't get a really hearty strike vote.

We dropped our money demands to seven and a half percent for a one-year term. Then the university made a second money offer. They upped the bonus from $200 to $400, the jerks. That was the first part of a two-year contract, and four percent for the second year. We asked the mediator to sign out. Which means we were preparing to hit the bricks. We didn't figure he was about to do any more good.

We didn't go all out. Because we didn't have a strong strike vote, we were in a position where not only did we have to negotiate with the university, but we had to sort of negotiate with the membership too. We started rotating job action, which means that we pulled specific areas. For instance, at the beginning of December 1978 we pulled the registrar's office. And we were hoping throughout this rotating job action to affect the university as much as possible, and the students and faculty as little as possible. So we pulled out areas like the bursar's office so they couldn't pay their bills, and the computing centre so they couldn't generate all their paper. We tried to go for the throat and heart. (Laughs.) We didn't pull out the departmental offices, so that teaching could go on. Our argument wasn't with the teaching staff.

This is the way it worked. We would pull out maybe twenty percent of the membership, and the rest of the membership would be levied twenty percent of their wages. That way everybody got eighty percent of their wages.

In the short term that's okay. Everybody is kind of happy. People aren't experiencing too many hardships. On eighty percent you can do okay for a while.

But the other side used to put out propaganda and say we weren't affecting anything, that everything was rolling right along. We talked to some supervisors, who happened to be decent people, and they told us things were actually chaos, absolutely looney tunes in the various areas where the workers had been pulled. Obviously. What were we doing there if we're not being effective by pulling out? At the same time, we weren't quite effective enough.

Towards the middle of December the university made its first _real_ money offer, which was its third money offer after a year and a half. And that was two percent the first year and four percent the second.

So we met and dithered on for a while. We dropped the reduction of the workforce article in an attempt to get a better percentage increase. We dropped our medical and dental premium demands from one hundred percent premium coverage down to fifty percent for medical and seventy percent for dental.

This is the nitty-gritty stuff of bargaining. There are people out of work, and there's five women sitting around making decisions that are going to affect the lives of 650 people and their families. The burden of that responsibility is incredible. We had never done it before, none of us. We didn't always know whether we were doing the right thing.

Because of our status of being independent and non-affiliated, we had no access to the kind of information that would be fairly readily available to a union that was affiliated with a national union, like CUPE, which has a really good research department. If you need information on wage rates, they plug it into a computer and spit it out the other end and give it to you. We used to have to do vast amounts of figuring, running around, going to the labour research bureau and doing our own research on contracts — this in addition to our Saturday strategy sessions and the gruelling process of negotiation itself. It was scary to have that kind of responsibility.

At the same time, we were starting to acquire a consciousness that made us more radical than the membership, and made us wonder if we were still in a position to be truly representative of them. We were starting to learn about the Board of Governors — like a board of directors that makes all the big decisions on campus — that has on its membership two executive officers of the Employers' Council of B.C., bosses of unorganized women workers in all those huge downtown office towers, who make maybe $850 a month. And it is in *their* interests not to allow us to have a decent increase.

This whole realization was dawning on us at the same time as all the hard bargaining was being done. And we started asking the question: "Are we in a position to be truly representative of these 650 people?" And not really knowing whether we absolutely were or weren't, but doing the best we could, struggling along, feeling really tired and overworked and sometimes unappreciated by the membership. And no doubt the membership thought — in fact I got this back every once in a while — that the contract committee was setting itself up as some kind of august body.

Until the beginning of March we had been pulling out members on rotating job action. Then the university started locking people out. They locked out people in the library, which is the area that serves students and faculty. We had been trying to be very careful not to affect the learning process, and the *first thing* they do is put out the library workers, the very heart 'of the university!

Oh God, they're pigs! The library is the shit-hole of the university as far as working conditions are concerned. It has the worst labour-management relations internally of anywhere. Almost every president of our union, as well as a lot of executive members, has come from the library. That's directly proportional to the amount of shit and hassles you get when you work in the library.

So they lock out the library. Besides being the most radicalized section of the bargaining unit, the library accounts for quite a large portion of the membership. So now we weren't looking at a twenty percent levy, it was getting up to thirty-five percent. We had a number of fairly frantic meetings. Two other areas voted that if any of their people got locked out, they would all go out.

And the university did it, they locked out more people. So rather than be levied to death for God knows how long, at fifty percent of our wages, we decided to pull the pin. We went out March 8 and stayed out until mid-April.

I really radicalized around both the strike and all of the side issues. We had eighteen people arrested on our picket line on March 22 and I got involved in the defence campaign for those people.

The students had called a rally in support of striking workers. There were a number of labour dignitaries and student society representatives, a speaker from AUCE, and it was a lovely day. I can remember feeling all warm and summery, even though it was March. There were lots of people there, probably three or four hundred in a very small area. We were down "at the lights," as we called it, the only entrance to the university. John Fryer from the B.C. Government Employees' Union told the crowd, "If this is going to be an effective picket line, we have to stop people from going through it. Period. Let's get out and block the road." And people were excited, enthusiastic, and feeling pretty happy, probably because of the sunshine more than anything else.

So off they went. And there were several hundred people blocking the road completely for some time. Traffic backed up. The RCMP came. The traffic backed up some more. The RCMP attempted to break up the line by forming a wedge and pushing people out of the way and letting cars through. They did this maybe three times, and they weren't particularly successful. This went on for about three hours. Fryer left about twenty minutes after it started. Nobody thought it was illegal.

They'd arrested one person early on and taken him off in a paddy wagon. And then, close to an hour later, they rushed the crowd and started hauling people away.

There had been a PA system on a flatbed truck. They cut it off without warning. An MC had been directing the crowd, urging people to keep control, not to do anything rash, to keep the picket line moving. They cut her off and rushed the picketers. They hauled away eighteen people. Some were students. Fourteen were members of various other unions.

First of all, they were charged with obstructing a police officer. A month later they were charged with obstructing the highway. And instead of taking this whole issue to the LRB (Labour Relations Board), which is the body where such infractions are normally referred, it was sent to the courts.

This was the first indication I had that the government had a certain role to play in labour-management disputes.

Then, instead of being charged with misdemeanours, they were charged with *criminal* offenses. And the trials were set individually, even though the eighteen people had been arrested at exactly the same place and time, over the very same alleged infractions. In the end we had to raise $20,000 to pay for these trials.

And during this whole process of going to trial after trial after trial, it became clear to me that not only do the bosses lie, and not only does the government lie and cheat but the police do too. It's a very radicalizing experience.

I mean, they made up these stories about the aggressiveness of the picketers towards them. According to them this gentle friend of mine flailed his way through the crowd, throwing police out of the way. Well, he just didn't do any such thing. And the crowd wasn't aggressive. It was happy and enthusiastic. They made up all this stuff to get convictions.

We were on strike almost six weeks when the membership voted to go for an industrial inquiry commission, a type of binding arbitration without calling it that. It's generally used in labour disputes that involve a great deal of violence on the picket line.

We had to negotiate the terms of the IIC. Normally the commissions are composed of one person, and that person is agreed to by both parties. But our lawyer suggested we go for a three-person commission because then we would get to appoint one nominee, they would get to appoint another nominee, and, hopefully, the third person would be slightly fair. You have a better chance of a fair hearing with a three-person set-up.

So at this point the intrepid AUCE 2 negotiating committee met with the B.C. Minister of Labour. It happened that our chairperson was sick the day we met with him to talk about this, so I did it. In we go, wide-eyed and bushy-tailed, and argue like mad for this three-person set-up. Well, they finally agree. So I phoned up Leo, our lawyer, a little later in the day and said, "Well, we got it." And he said, "That's great!" He sounded almost too excited about it, so I asked why. And he said there's only ever been one three-person commission before. And I thought, holy shit. If he had told us before that we were going for a real precedent, we probably would have all stayed home sick. (Laughs.)

We did everything by the ass of our pants, sort of. There we go not knowing what the perils are, so being quite brave and quite determined and quite feisty. But not because we knew the whole story, not because we knew the ramifications of everything we ever tried to do. It was really a kind of blind courage. (Laughs.)

So then we did decide on the terms. We agreed that the commission would deal with the wages and the vacation work agreement. The last time there had been a strike, the university had tried to get tricky by allowing temps to finish terms, things like that. So we got a very good, tight return-to-work agreement.

Towards the end of April 1979 we went back to work. The commission didn't meet until August. Sometime between going back to work and August we learned we had to produce a brief for the IIC. We thought, oh well, a brief. Then we found out that these briefs are usually extremely comprehensive and could be several hundred pages long. So then the contract committee had to set about producing this thing. (Laughs.)

We pooled our collective resources. The chairperson, Norma, wrote the wages section. Another woman wrote the equal pay for work of equal value section. I wrote the history section. Norma and I both took at least a week off work — the union paid us — so it could get written, edited and typed, folded together and proofread and all the rest of it. In the end it was about 300 pages long. The university's was about forty.

Then we went off to the IIC hearing. It didn't take very long, five sessions at most. Our nominee was a wonderful woman named Diane MacKenzie, who fought for us very hard, and we managed to get the vacation scheduling clause. That was good. Our wages position was based on the equal pay for work of equal value argument. And the commission said they couldn't possibly address the question of justice, it wasn't within the parameters of their jurisdiction. Clearly they weren't interested in giving us equal pay for work of equal value with a six percent increase in the first year and one percent in the second, when inflation was running at ten or eleven percent a year.

It was binding on both sides. And that's what we ended up with.

We've learned a lot of lessons. But we've never had a chance to consistently define the lessons so that the next negotiation team can learn from them, doesn't go in cold the way we did. We didn't know how to go for an IIC. We didn't know how to go for a mediator. We didn't know which forms to use. We didn't really know how to conduct strike votes. The provincial organization didn't know any of this stuff either, because the provincial is only one paid person trying to service five locals on a day-to-day basis. She didn't have the information or the time to get all the stuff we needed. You need information and you need it now. You can't fool around. But things were muddled, really muddled.

We need to do a balance sheet, to go through the documents, such as the minutes of the negotiations. But some of them never got typed because I didn't have time. There's fourteen pages of longhand minutes, and my handwriting is almost illegible. It was absolutely critical that at some point along the way we sit down and say, "Here's what we did right; here's what we did wrong. Here are the consequences of doing something right. We rattle the chains a little bit, and they do this. We rattle the chains a little bit more and they do this."

During our strike, for instance, we threatened to shut down UBC (University of British Columbia). Well, when we threatened that, suddenly the B.C. Fed (B.C. Federation of Labour) called a meeting and all the unions from UBC came and we put forward our position and suddenly the Minister of Labour stepped in. You do something, they respond. Cause and effect, dialectics.

But we've never been able to codify those kinds of lessons. Everything is continuing to be passed on by word of mouth. We simply don't have the time, the money, the personnel, to get that stuff written down. And the provincial office is in no better situation as far as I can make out. So when AUCE Local 1 went on strike last year, there was no way for them to liaise with us around certain basic issues. We could see them repeating all our mistakes. It's nuts!

If we don't do something to get stronger, and in my opinion the only way to do that is to merge with another existing union, then we're going to get squashed. It's a big issue for us now, whether to affiliate with the CLC.

The universities have a national organization that stretches from coast to coast. They had a convention at Simon Fraser last fall, and I sort of drifted by and swiped their documents and looked through them. They have lists of every single post-secondary institution in this country, broken down by whether they have a union, what kind of union, when was the last strike, how long did it last, what were the issues. They've got a national organization that is gathering together information that is going to help them fight us and win. Right?

We don't have access to that kind of co-ordinated information, that kind of co-ordinated assistance. It seems to me that when you're a worker, you're subject to the whims of a whole lot of levels of bosses. You have the boss, you have the bosses' organizations, you have government intervention — all of these factors which seem to me to shift quite heavily against the strength of a union. And when you're talking about a union that doesn't have any ties, any links, and you're talking about a union that has undergone a number of fairly serious economic setbacks in the way of strikes, then you're talking about a balance of forces that doesn't bode well for our very existence, let alone the growth of AUCE.

Joan has multiple sclerosis and was forced to stop work in 1981. "I've kissed the contract many times," she told me over the phone. "We negotiated a good, long-term disability clause. Thank God for that. As it is, I have a livable guaranteed monthly income; otherwise, I'd be shit out of luck." As energy permits, Joan is active in social movements including the B.C. Organization to Fight Racism, and Socialist Challenge. She helped to organize the national conference Women and Words/Les Femmes et Les Mots, held in B.C. last summer.

H*eavy duty equipment mechanic Leni Balaban*
Edmonton, Alberta

PULLING WRENCHES

LENI BALABAN

I

N SEPTEMBER 1980 I took part in the first national Women in
Trades Conference in Winnipeg. I was in my hotel room one
evening when someone knocked on my door. I answered to find a
woman wearing a stylish print dress, high-heeled shoes and large
hoop earrings, her long hair pinned up on top of her head.

Someone from the conference had told her I would be interested
in her story for my book, she said. "I'm a Caterpillar mechanic,"
she explained. Another stereotype bit the dust.

Ten days later I interviewed Leni at her home in Edmonton,
surrounded by paintings, crocheted cushions and other samples of
her handiwork. After we spoke, she showed me her current project, a refurbished and gleaming 1948 Plymouth in the drive-

−155−

way. She was obviously a woman with a lot of guts and many talents.

I CAME FROM A European background. My mother was East German, my father Russian. We came to Canada just after the war. We were DP's, displaced people, and we immigrated to Canada.

My parents always worked. My father worked in hospitals as an orderly. My mother was a steady night nurse. She'd come home in the morning, pack us off to school, sleep during the day. When we'd come home we'd wake her up, and she'd be with us all evening. Then she'd pack us off to bed and off to work she'd go. My father would be working either mornings or afternoons, so the kids were never left alone. We learned at an early age to fend for ourselves, to become independent. That was actively encouraged.

My mother was always trying to push me to go into botany. She had this thing. She wanted to study it herself and she was trying to do it through me. She was a very, very domineering person. Extremely domineering. She wasn't happy with my father, and as a result, there was quite a bit of strain in the house when we were growing up.

I resisted my mother all the way down the line, even as a kid. I was always on the chubby side, though never obese. She was always trying to dress me up in chiffon, all those fancy things that were just totally unsuited to my personality and appearance. It got to the point where, when my mother tried to tell me something, I knew automatically that if I did the opposite, I could not go wrong; whereas if I did what she tried to advise me, it was invariably a mistake. (Laughs.)

My mother was a very competent, capable and highly gifted woman. She taught us an awful lot. She taught me how to use my hands, and I think I'd die if anything ever happened to my hands, because everything I do depends on them. I mean *everything!* Music, job, creativity — you name it. Everything in this room I've made. I love tinkering and rebuilding old cars.

I had three sisters, and every one of us is a very strong individual. We're all into different things. We're all very creative. We all play musical instruments. We're all very assertive. My little sister went through a stage where she believed that you're supposed to lean on a man, and she picked up a weak one. When she leaned on him she was disappointed, and finally she smartened up. The rest of us all stood on our own two feet. We're all very independent minded. Sometimes I wish we hadn't been quite so much.

I learned some valuable things at home, but I also learned I wanted to get the hell out of there as soon as I was old enough. Which I did.

I went to Lakehead University and took the two-year forest technology program. At that time it was very difficult for girls to get a job in a non-traditional field such as forestry, unless you wanted to work for the government in the research lab. I was only the second woman to be in the course, and was the only one in a class of forty-five men. They were real macho. Same as the engineers at the university. Big heavy boozing, gruff and rude, an ignorant image to maintain. It made it pretty rotten. It bothered me a lot at the time. I guess I wasn't quite mature enough to just say, "The hell with it."

We learned everything about trees. I mean everything. How to measure the diameter and calculate the volume of available timber, mapping from aerial photography and other things. People that graduated were able to hire on as technicians with private companies. With an additional law enforcement course, if you were male, you could become a game warden. Women were actively discouraged from that. Like everything else, they tried to direct you into jobs they thought would be suitable for you instead of letting you make up your own mind. Same old thing. (Laughs.)

Right after I finished, I married a geologist who was put in charge of a mine up in northern Manitoba, about eighty miles in the bush east of Flin Flon.

We were extremely isolated. There was no road in, only the railroad. The train went five days a week, a local ore run. There were 110 men and two other women out at camp. One of the women was the mine foreman's wife. She was hardly ever there, always in town. The other one was the cook.

I had no job, which just about drove me stark bananas. There was some nonsense about women not being allowed underground in the mine, but I think in Manitoba even then — that was eleven years ago — you could get a job underground if you pushed it. But they said there was nothing available. Then there was an opening in the kitchen, so I learned to wash dishes and how to camp cook, just to keep my sanity and make a few extra dollars. I made $450 a month, with only two days off.

The cook I was working for was always trying to tell me how good I had it, what a wonderful man I'd married, and I shouldn't want more. I should be content with being Mrs. Bigshot.

We stuck it out there for a year. My husband was very ambitious, and it was very important for him to get ahead with his work. Everything else was incidental. That was his prime concern, and the longer I was with him, the more I realized just how vitally important his career was to him.

It was his very first job, fresh out of university, and he was over there at the mine sometimes until ten o'clock at night on his maps. And he asked me if I could just bear with him, because it was his first crack at getting established in something. Here he was given this mine to develop, which some people with five year's experience weren't even given. I accepted that.

Then he was offered another prize job up in the Yukon, as a geologist. It was 200 miles northwest of Whitehorse on the Alaska Highway. He was doing the same kind of work there, developing the mine, putting in the same long hours, seven days a week. Which meant no time off.

And again, no job for me. They had surveyors there — underground engineer type surveyors — and were running through them at the rate of about one a year. They went through nine of them. So I asked the mine foreman if I could have a job, because I had surveying qualifications from my forestry background. "Oh, we can't do that. The men might be embarrassed." I got so mad I even went as far as Whitehorse to ask for a job. I had one interview at Manpower. "Well, we have some chambermaids' jobs, but you probably wouldn't break even if you had to pay rent on a place. Besides, what would happen if you got the maternal urge?" I had to give him a blast. It got me really angry, really mad.

I decided to go back to university and finish off my degree in arts, because with my background I could get some credits. I went back to Thunder Bay. My husband was going to come down for Thanksgiving, for the weekend. Then all of a sudden: "I don't know whether I can or not" — after he'd been up there a whole year without a holiday. By that time my nerves were at the point where I couldn't keep on at university anymore. So after a month I got my tuition refunded and I got the hell back up there. By this time I was ready for a nervous breakdown. My self-image was shot. I couldn't get a job. My husband was married to *his* job, nothing was going right. They put me in the hospital for a few days to calm me down, and of course I got the usual dose of Valium for a nervous breakdown.

It was one of those classic company towns, places where women just haven't got anything to do, and I just didn't know how to cope with it.

The housing was supplied by the company, all expenses paid except for groceries which were horrendously high even then. Then they started to import all these people, and I have never seen such an unhappy, bitchy bunch of backstabbing, miserable people. I saw more marriages go under, a lot of tension. The people up there, there was just no getting along with them. Nobody got along with anybody. It was really bad. Alcoholism. The saddest thing.

I felt completely and utterly powerless. I got to the point of being hooked on Valium. I'd get up in the morning about eleven o'clock. I'd go lie in the bathtub until about three o'clock in the afternoon. I'd get my ass out of the bathtub, cook supper and then eat three quarters of it before my husband got home, out of boredom. And then by seven o'clock I was asleep again. I weighed 185 pounds. I was grossly unhappy as well as grossly fat. So I finally decided, Hey girl, that's enough. You can't put up with this shit much longer. I told my husband, "We're leaving or *I'm* leaving. I'm not putting up with this any longer. I'm tired of not having anything to do or any say in what's happening to my future. Now, what are we going to do?" He says, "Okay, I'll give my notice."

So we got transferred back to northern Manitoba again, to the same old mining camp. By this time the relationship was starting to lose a lot of interest for me. (Laughs.) I didn't quite want to admit it, but I realized that if I was single, at least I would be free to choose for myself.

I worked in the kitchen again for awhile. Same old cook, same hassles. Then this store came up for sale, the camp commissary, a little shack, and I bought it. All I did was buy my stock — soap, cigarettes, laundry soap, shaving gear — and I had no overhead, so I made about four hundred dollars a month clear profit, for working two or three hours a day. This worked out quite fine.

I did that for about a year. Then I got a job in one of the hotels in the nearest town, thirty miles away. I was cooking during the day, and slinging beer in the beer parlour on Saturday night. I made twenty, thirty dollars a day in tips. I had an apartment in town and my own snow machine in winter so I could always run back and forth to camp. But my marriage was deteriorating even further.

I had heard there were technician's jobs with Churchill Forest Industries in The Pas. I decided, "No harm lost," and I went down there and applied for a job. They said, "Well, no, we haven't got openings, and we have several other applicants on file." But they had a bush camp up by Wabowden, about 130 miles from Snow Lake up towards Thompson. They were so desperate for people that they said, "Can you show up for work in two weeks with a power saw?"

I had no qualms about being far away from my husband. Nuts to that.

The first day I showed up I had this old Pioneer 650 chainsaw that I picked up for fifty dollars. Those things — well, a 250-pound logger would have trouble holding one. They're extremely heavy. The camp foreman took one look and his mouth dropped open. He was too polite to laugh in my face. (Laughs.) He put me on the skidder — a tractor vehicle, rubber tired, articulated steering, with a winch on the back, that hauls bundles of wood out to piles along the roadside. I knew how to drive a standard car, and I knew a little bit about engines, that sort of thing. But for some reason I was awfully clumsy on that machine. It was something completely unfamiliar. Of course, the foreman figured I'd never make it anyhow, so he said, "There's a job opening in the kitchen. Maybe we'll put you in there for a little while." I figured, "Well, the pay is awfully good. I'm meeting people." There was one girl I made good friends with up there. I couldn't complain. I was on my own. I was actually getting a paycheque. And within thirty days of hiring, if I kept my mouth shut and watched what I was doing, I'd be in the union and then I could squawk to get back in the bush.

So I did it that way. I took the job in the kitchen, and as soon as my thirty days were up I was in the union, the International Woodworkers of America.

There was something in our contract that allowed you to take a leave of absence for educational purposes. So again I went to The Pas, and this time I applied to get into a heavy equipment operating course. I figured I might not learn how to operate these machines on the job, but I'd know by the time I got back.

You needed two qualifications to take that course. One was a grade eight education, which I had, and the other was a valid Manitoba chauffeur's licence, which I also had. They tried to tell me they'd have to give me a mechanical aptitude test. I said, "Oh, you do, eh? Fine. Then you're going to have to tell me which one of the male applicants for the course had to take that aptitude test too. If I have to take it, you'll have to prove to me that they had to take it too." That was it. Nothing more was said about it. So I was in the course. I learned an awful lot.

And when I went back into the bush, I fought to get back onto the equipment again. And slowly but surely I started to operate different types of equipment. One item was a harvester, like an excavator, a giant excavator on tracks. Instead of the bucket, it has a snipper head that cuts the trees and lays them in bunches. I got to be very proficient on that. And of course I was pretty rough on it. I used to break things, like hydraulic hoses.

One thing out there, they were *always* short of mechanics. If you had a good working relationship with a mechanic, you'd treat him as well as possible. No matter how green or dumb you were about pulling wrenches, you'd go out of your way to try to help him. Then if you did something foolish and screwed up, then he wouldn't shaft you with the foreman either. It worked out okay. I got even more fascinated with pulling wrenches. I thought, Well, that's something I'd like to pursue seriously sometime in the future.

On the job itself, now there I had hassles. "What are you doing here? You shouldn't be working here. We don't approve of this. We don't approve of that." And the foremen! I had enough sense to keep my yap shut until I was in the union. And then when they started to threaten things, like putting me back to work in the kitchen, I was able to tell them, "Try it, buddy." I developed an awful thick skin, but there were times when I came home on Friday and cried all weekend. Then I'd go back to work again.

It wasn't so much that I was trying to prove something, but the important thing was it was a good job. It paid well, and it gave me some of my self-respect back. The hassles I figured were worth it, just so I could have a measure of independence. They were the price I was paying for it.

My husband got transferred from Snow Lake to Flin Flon. He bought a house, and I went there on weekends.

By this time my marriage was . . . it wasn't happy to go home. I'd come home to that house and we'd fight over everything. I couldn't stand it, but I didn't have the nerve to say, "This relationship isn't working." There was one incident that was it for me and I should have realized it right there.

I was out at camp, without a vehicle. I was going to get a ride in to Flin Flon to go for a beer and movie Wednesday night, and I told my husband I'd call to tell him if I had a ride or not.

On the way, there was a terrible accident that six of us got into, and we ended up rolling twice into a ditch, ending up in swamp water. I put one elbow through the windshield and cracked the other shoulder. We hitched a ride up to Thompson, about eighty miles, to get to hospital. We looked half dead, blood all over the place. I was about the worst hurt, though I wasn't in too bad shape. Finally about eleven o'clock at night they got through with patching us up and X-raying me and telling me I was going to be okay but to take it easy. I phoned my husband and apologized for being late. "I've been in a car accident and I'm not hurt badly, but I'm in great pain. Do you think there's any way you can come down to get me?" He said, "I can't take the time off work."

It sounds like I'm making him out to be the villain and he's not, because there were lots of things I'd fallen down on too. I didn't always make as much of an effort as I should have to understand him either.

I hated Flin Flon. I hated it as much as I had hated the Yukon. We had a shack of a house. And of course the smelter was at the other end of town. We'd open the window and smell all the sulphur dioxide and choke on it. I must have had a negative attitude, but I couldn't see any redeeming features about that place that could make me stand to be there for any length of time.

My husband got transferred to Thunder Bay. He took a leave of absence to go back to university for his master's in business administration. I got a job in a bush camp in northern Ontario where I knew they were hiring women.

I was making trailer payments, paying for two cars. Then it just got intolerable. I met someone in the bush camp and had an affair. I told my husband about it. This was it. He said, "It's okay. I had one in Flin Flon too." "Well, you bastard. You couldn't even be honest with me. At least I've had the decency to be honest."

So that was it. We split up. I figured I'd make the payments on the trailer and things like that. He had supported me for all those years because I was incapable of getting a job. So I figured I'd do it for now.

I got a job working up at the Great Lakes Paper Company with eight other women in the bush camp — it was fantastic! I made some good and close friends that I'm still in touch with. I was operating heavy equipment. We all were. And I've never seen eight women that could stick together like that. An insult against one was an insult against all. We didn't take shit from anybody.

The district supervisor there was the absolute worst. If we'd had the law on our side in 1975 the way we do now, we could have hauled him into court for sexual harassment. Except that he probably would've blackballed us at the other camps. He was a real pervert, sick in the head. He'd take these polaroid pictures of some of the pin-up floozies from *Hustler* magazine. He'd pass them around at the other camps and say, "This is one of the girls from 603 (the number of our camp)." They used to call it the Great Lakes Whorehouse. Now if that's not sexual harassment, I don't know what is.

He also did his best to find boys sneaking in and out of the women's bunkhouse. Not that there was any sneaking done. There were three girls who had a steady man. They were with them whenever they went to town on weekends. They had a living relationship. And they figured that they were allowed visiting privileges up at the camp. The camp foreman tried to stop that until we hollered, "Union!"

The union wasn't very strong down there. It was the Lumber and Saw Mill Workers. It was better than nothing, though. We went through some rough times. There was time off because of a stupid strike. We were off work for five weeks. I went back to Wabowden and got my old job back while the strike was on. Then I came back to the Great Lakes and worked until spring.

They have a general three-week layoff in the spring, when the ground thaws out. They can't haul wood 'cause the roads are shut down. That year the Ministry of Natural Resources was giving a scaling course at Pembroke, Ontario. A scaler measures wood, and you have to be government licensed and approved. I was promised the job of scaler in the camp if I got that licence. So I figured I'd take the plunge, and I went to Pembroke for the course.

Scaling is a high paying job. It was a skill that was in great demand, so I figured I'd have no problem getting a job. I could have had my pick of a dozen jobs, I think. So I got my licence, went up to camp and scaled wood there for the rest of the summer.

Now that was running around. All I'd been doing before was punch a time clock and pull levers and grease my machine all day, and all of a sudden I was responsible for 80,000 cords of wood a year which had to be measured and mapped. You have your company checking up on you to make sure you're accurate. My boss was a check scaler for the company, and then the government check scaler would come in every week and check on me too. I was allowed three percent leeway on whatever they came up with. We had to be accurate, because what the company paid on stumpage dues depended on my scaling.

Then in the fall the mill in town was going to go on strike, and I thought, "I've had enough of this strike bullshit. These idiots are getting good money. They don't even know what they're striking for." I decided I was going to look for another job. I thought I'd take a crack at doing mapping, road layout work, just maybe I could get into supervision. Imagine having that on my job record. I would impress potential employers.

I went to Caramat, about 250 miles northeast of Thunder Bay, and was there for two years. I got treated extremely well there. You couldn't ask for better people to work with.

My social life wasn't the best. There were lots of families there, lots of wives. Women in the kitchen, but none in the bush. It was again the typical one-horse town, the same bush camp mentality. The women were down on somebody who was a little bit different, who lived independently. And a lot of the men too. They'd say, "You're always trying to prove you're better." I said, "Prove it? What is there to prove? I think I proved it a long time ago. I'm capable of acting like a responsible adult and holding down a job."

So the social life was not the best, but something I could cope with. Some of the people that I socialized with drank fairly heavily. There's an awful lot of drinking that goes on in these bush towns. It's one of the few things to do. I kept busy with other things. I had my activities and my hobbies. But then, you know, you want some company, and after a while you get caught up in all the saucing. I did more than my share of it. There were times when I started losing respect for myself.

So after I was there for a year and a half they put me on as a relief foreman. And that's when the fun began. They put me on bossing a cut and skid crew of twenty-one, which included a bulldozer operator and a mechanic. The Cat man you never had to worry about. The mechanic was a really good person, very capable of running his own show, a good guy to shoot the breeze with when it wasn't too busy. The rest of the men, there were a few who would just try to see what they could get away with. I was responsible for giving them their bonus, and they were supposed to tell me how many trees they cut. Now, having measured wood for two years, I knew a cord of wood when I saw one. And when a man said he cut fifty, sixty trees, and I knew he'd only put about thirty on the pile, I could tell and I'd give him a lot less. They found out quite smartly, because the bonus sheets were posted the next day, that they weren't going to get away with that. They did some hollering, "I'll call my supervisor who's also got a scaling licence. We'll see what he says."

And when the men found out they couldn't cheat me, that I'd stomp on them real hard, there were no more problems. My attitude was, I'll treat them with respect, like grown-ups, until they prove otherwise, and then I'll get tough with them.

It was a pretty interesting summer. One thing the company didn't know, and I wasn't going to tell them until a month before I left, was that I had decided to go back to an old love, which was pulling wrenches.

I applied to Sault College for the heavy duty mechanic course and got accepted. So I took the course, as usual the only woman in it. People kind of gawked a bit. But that was all right. My instructors were very, very supportive of me down there. My classmates were good to deal with. I met Joe, my husband, there too. He was in one of the other classes.

When I got finished the course, I saw Manpower about landing a job. By this time Joe and I were engaged. I didn't want to go back to the bush camps. But the counsellor was trying to tell me that I had to go because there weren't any openings elsewhere. He started to lay on this lecture: "People like you should be grateful for a job." I said, "Listen, buster, I was making $18,000 a year and I quit that job to take up this. I'll be making more than you as a first year mechanic. So don't hand me that bullshit." He was trying to intimidate me and I wasn't going to take it.

You're allowed government money for an exploratory (looking for apprenticeships in other parts of the country). I got an offer to apply for work at Angus in Edmonton, a Caterpillar dealer. I went out and applied for mechanic apprentice, and they hired me within two weeks. That made me feel good, because there were only openings for about eighty people, and they had over 600 applicants that year. I figured it's a promising thing when they treat me like that. They probably checked me out more closely than the men, but I passed the grades. No sweat.

Joe and I came out here together. He quit his job in Ontario. We knew that under the circumstances with his being male and having more experience, he'd have his pick of jobs out here. Since I had a chance out here, he came too, and we got married shortly after that.

I started a four-year apprenticeship in 1978. Next June I'll have my time in. I'll be a licensed heavy duty mechanic with an interprovincial certification, I hope.

At Angus I service Caterpillars. Angus is the only official Caterpillar dealer for Alberta. We do all the warranty work, and anybody who brings in Caterpillar machines to sell in the province has to be Angus certified. There are about 500 mechanics altogether.

I've been treated very, very well. I've gotten my fair, if not more fair, set of chances. There were times I should have got my ass reamed out a little more for being careless. But they didn't. The foreman was a bit nervous about giving me too much shit. Sometimes I felt that I deserved it. I enjoyed not getting it! (Laughs.) But I knew that sometimes he would have been a little bit harder on a man.

There was one foreman I had a bit of a problem with in the beginning. He was an old-country type person, set in his ways, and just not used to women on the job. But once we got our differences worked out, it was all right. We respected each other.

We have some women in the parts department but no others on the floor. It took the men about a year and a half before they started to talk to me. Which I expected. I wasn't too worried about it. Because I had somebody to talk to when I came home. I think that I mightn't have been so tolerant if I hadn't had so much support at home. That made an awful difference.

It's nice to have someone in the same trade, the same racket. It's really good. We generally have a half-hour to an hour before supper, going over the job, rebuilding whatever we did, swearing about those good-for-nothings, how stupid it was if it was a rough day, patting ourselves on the shoulder if we'd done a good job. After that, the job stays at work until the next day.

Now there's always somebody to shoot the breeze with at work too. You're working with somebody and you get to know who they are and where they're from, that kind of stuff. Coffee time. And of course you hear everybody start to talk cars and motorbikes. That's just up my alley. (Laughs.)

There are times when the job gets so incredibly dirty, so incredibly rough, that you sort of wonder what kind of masochist you are to put up with all this shit. What you do then is go outside the shop for about two minutes, take a breath of clean air to cool down, and then go back to it again. You'll get it eventually. The machines were built by people, and I've never met a machine that's stubborner than me yet. I keep that in mind. You have to be determined. Very determined.

Things don't go right. That happens all the time. It's part of the job. The job is rough. If the job were easy, there'd be a lot more mechanics. There's really nothing you can't master and learn to enjoy. There's certain types of machines I hate to work on because there's nothing easy about them. The bolts are almost impossible to get at. You skin your knuckles, lose your wrenches and have to buy new ones.

There's a story going around about the engineer who designs all these machines. He came home one day and found a mechanic in bed with his wife, and he's made it hard on us ever since. (Laughs.) And believe me that's so true. If some of those dummies pushing slide rules and calculators came down and tried things with a wrench, it would make things a lot better for us. Theoretically, it's supposed to work. But then, theoretically, bumble bees aren't supposed to fly. The bumble bees don't know that. So theoretically, a lot of things are supposed to be possible that just aren't. That's the biggest mechanics' complaint, and it's universal.

My other complaint is not major. See my fingers? That's after a shower and a bath. Your hands will never become clean unless you just about take a layer of skin off. Which I can live with. If you want to play elegant, you can stick false fingernails on.

My hair is long. It's a little bit impractical where I am. I mean, automotive nuts are bad, but heavy duty where I am, where you're under big machines with dirt and oil dripping, long hair is a little bit impractical. My shampoo bills are horrendously high. Fortunately the wages I make more than make up for it.

If I got pregnant, I'd refuse to quit work. I'd never stay home to raise a kid. I tried being a housewife and it just about drove me mad. It's not my style. So I'd have to find care for the baby. If I get pregnant, they can damn well give me light duty like they do the men sometimes. Angus is good that way. A man breaks his leg, has a skiing accident or something, they allow him to come back at full pay on light duty. They're in the office answering phones or running little errands. Which is really decent.

I think that probably the last four or five months I wouldn't be able to do much on the machines. Lifting is heavy. I can easily lift a hundred pounds safely, but I wouldn't want to try if I were pregnant. It would be easy to fall off the machines too. I jump off them all the time. It gets slippery. It's just not sensible. And some of the garbage you inhale, some of those fumes, I don't think would be the best for you. So you'd have to use common sense, take some precautions. But I don't think there'd be anything I couldn't handle.

I'll stick to it. Yesterday we had to get two machines out in a hurry. We'd been tinkering with them on Friday, but they had to be out Saturday. The customers were getting ready to pick them up. There wasn't in fact much left on it, but that machine was out, and you took it around the yard for a spin and tried it, and you knew that it was running as well as new. Every time that door closes behind one more, you feel good. You know there's no end in sight, of course, but you like to kid yourself that that was good. Get a sense of pride.

Leni received her papers as a journeyman mechanic and is still working at Angus repairing Caterpillars.

*S*teelworker Cathy Mulroy in the Copper Refinery,
International Nickel Company of Canada,
Sudbury, Ontario

MINER'S DAUGHTER

CATHY MULROY

I<small>T WAS A COLD</small> October afternoon. The Inco smokestack domi-
nated the landscape as we walked across the parking lot to the
copper refinery warehouse. Inside, it was dark and warm. A
supervisor joined us, gesturing across the empty space to a loading dock. A figure broke away from the workers there and saun-
tered across the floor towards us.

"Hiya," she said. She was younger and smaller than I expected, with a mass of hair flying out from her hardhat and an
ear-to-ear grin. In her tight overalls, safety glasses and boots, she
provided a striking contrast to the public relations lady who
accompanied us in make-up and high heels.

Cathy turned to the supervisor. "Well, are you going to put me
on the cast so they can take pictures or not?" The supervisor

looked uneasy. The challenge was obviously not a new one, but it was clear he'd rather not discuss it in front of us. They argued anyway, the supervisor citing safety rules, Cathy finally getting her way. She turned to us and winked heavily as we crossed the warehouse towards the area where molten copper is cast into moulds. She had enjoyed winning this skirmish.

Later that evening she talked to us at her kitchen table.

I'VE LIVED HERE in Sudbury all my life. I come from a family of five kids and one adopted; six altogether. I went to high school up to grade nine. I tried that twice. And then I got pregnant when I was sixteen years old, and because both of us came from such Roman Catholic backgrounds, we automatically got married. And so my parents made the arrangements, told me to be at the church at twelve o'clock on May first. And I was there. (Laughs.) Then I had my first child, a little boy, Pepe. We were very poor. I think Lloyd was making something like sixty-eight dollars a week. He was a printer at the university.

After Pepe got a little older, I decided to get a job somewhere because we weren't making enough money. I started working in a department store as a clerk. I got laid off because I refused to let my boss put up my curtains for me. (Laughs.) I bought some curtains and he insisted on coming to my house to put them up, while my husband was away. I said no, and got laid off.

Then I worked as a cashier at Canadian Tire, and I got laid off there for a similar type reason. I started at Silverman's, which is a department store that was run by very rich people. I didn't get along too well with the women there because I've always been an outspoken person. I got laid off because of cutbacks. I was nineteen.

Those were the only jobs available for women in Sudbury then: clerks, waitresses, bank tellers, behind the cash register, babysitting. There weren't even real estate or sales ladies around at that time. There was nothing for women.

I was putting up wallpaper at home one day when Trudeau came on the television and said Inco would be hiring women. So I said, "What the hell. What can I lose?" It was 1974, the year before International Women's Year. The reason they had to hire was so that they would look good that year. So I went down there and applied and got the job, right off the bat. I went in for the hell of it. I didn't expect to get a job, let alone a good job. That had never even dawned on me.

Another thing is that when you're working in a mining town, you have a lot of pride about being a miner's daughter. My dad worked forty-one years for the company. I remember sitting on his knee watching Red Skelton on television, and when he had to work afternoons I would just hurt in my heart because he wouldn't be watching it and I knew how much he liked Red Skelton. You'd hear the blast at four o'clock and know he was there. God, it would shake the whole earth. Windows would rattle. The trains used to come right through town. Black smoke all the way. The pollution was so bad you could cut it with a knife. And I always worried about my dad being in the mines.

When I started working there, I realized all the dangerous things my dad used to go through. They put me on the cast, the hoist that you saw me on today. That's where they pour molten copper into moulds. As each one solidifies, you pick it up with a manually-controlled air hoist — it weighs six to seven hundred pounds — and swing it over to the water tanks where it's cooled. I'd been there about six weeks when it broke on its way down. It weighs about twelve hundred pounds. It came towards me, hitting me in the side. And I went flying backwards, and that's how I found out I was pregnant. I was rushed to hospital where they took a blood test and came back about twenty minutes later to tell me I was pregnant. My reaction was: "What! From the hoist? Compensation!" (Laughs.)

I'd figured the reason I hadn't started my period was because of the atmosphere. You know, different job, the tension and everything else. So I never really thought about it. But because I was hit by the hoist and they couldn't take X-rays, Compensation had to pay all the time I was pregnant. That was the beginning. (Shakes her head.)

Six weeks after I had the baby I went back to work on the cast. I stayed there for a long, long time. And shitty jobs? Like you wouldn't believe. They'd put you on this job called cleaning the pit. I used to get that job after every cast. All the shit and excess that fell off the ladles, all the extra molten metal that fell on the floor and hardened up. There would be piles and piles of it. Nothing ever works there. So you'd have to shovel it out.

Cleaning beside the furnaces, that was a really bad job. You'd have to get all the copper that fell on the floor from behind the furnaces, and it was so hot in there that your jeans would stick to you. I mean they'd just be fire hot, eh? And it was a mistake to wear them too tight, because you'd have to cool them off by pulling on them.

They wanted to get rid of us women. They didn't want us there. The men were so threatened. They're still threatened, even after six years. They used to say, "What do you think you're doing here, anyways? This is no place for a woman. This is a man's job. Don't you know that you're taking away a man's job? A man has to support his family. And you're taking that away from somebody." And I'd think, "Well, maybe I am. Maybe I'd better start thinking about this." But then I'd think, "Well, jeez, I'm supporting a family too. I'm here because I've got grade nine education, and most men that work in Sudbury with that education work in the mines, so why can't I?"

I'd get phone calls, threatening phone calls, like: "If you don't get off that job, something just might happen." Really horrid things. Drunks would call and say, "Just you wait. We'll get you for taking this job." Wives. Oh, jeez, wives would call, especially if I went for a drink with the guys after work. They'd call my husband and say, "Your wife is drinking beer with my husband." And when I'd get home he'd be all in an uproar.

Some men were friendly, though. They'd say, "What are you working so hard for? Come and sit down in the lunch room." But the three of us who were placed in the anode (where copper is cast) thought, "Oh, we can't go in the lunch room; it's not break time." But if your work is finished, why not? We didn't think of it that way, though. And we worked, and we worked, and we worked. We worked all the hours we were there; we'd take our half-hour for lunch and half-hour for coffee.

At first I isolated myself. I tried to stay away from the men as much as possible. I just wanted them to know me as their co-worker, not as Cathy. Now, most of them know me as Cathy. I'm their friend or their daughter or their sister, part of the family that's there.

But at first they used to watch you constantly, every little thing you did. And you don't get respect for nothing; you have to earn respect. Once you've earned it, it's not usually lost, because you fought for it by standing up for yourself, handling your own load, by being honest and open with people. Working side by side, backing men up if they had a problem, just being their friend. That helped. If they can't handle it, they're no good to you anyway.

Sometimes I'd be shovelling, and because I got really bad stomach problems — first gallstones and then a hiatus hernia — the next load was going to be the last. But the guys would come along and give me a hand because they knew about my health. Others, of course, they wouldn't, but there was always somebody around. I'd do the same for them.

Another thing was, a lot of the guys cheered me on some-times. There was this one job called "skimming the furnace" which is a really hard, hard job. You had to lift the ravel, this gigantic pole which looks like a rake without picks. It's just solid. And you'd stick it in the copper and skim the top off. There would be chunks and bricks floating around in there, you name it. I decided to give it a try.

I couldn't even lift the ravel up, that's how heavy it is. And you have to soap it up so it slides along this bar while you skim. The guys lifted it up for me. A guy gave me spats, asbestos things you tie around your feet. I must have looked like a robot, because I'm only five-foot-one. And I got one there and started to skim, and believe me it was like pulling a train.

It was graveyard shift, and the guys started coming out of the lunch room. And they lined up on the tracks right beside where I was skimming, and they were chanting: "Go, go, go, go." It just made me want to do it all the more. I felt like the Hulk. I had that inner energy. And I just did it. And finally when my pot was full they went: "Yay! Yay!" Clapping on the tracks. And I turned to the foreman, proud, and I said, "I knew I could do it."

The guys were there. If you really needed them, they were there. You gotta tap into the solidarity. It's there. It's just that you've gotta get in it, or it will be superficial. They're afraid to talk to you because you're a woman, afraid to say things because they don't know how you're going to take it. Once they know you well, that's all broken down. They can say anything to me now — pretty well. But now they never, ever talk about my body. Before, it was constant. I don't even wear a bra at work anymore; I wear T-shirts. And I'll be damned if they'll tell me to wear one because I have breasts. If I have to wear one, every fat man in there's going to have to wear one, too. (Laughs.)

I've got this thing about foremen being little Hitlers in the world. That's what they're like. They used to follow me around when I first worked there. If I went to the washroom they used to stand at the bottom of the stairs. And of course I was scared. I didn't know what to say. One day I decided to have lunch with the women, which I wasn't supposed to do because they were eating up in the dry (change room), which we weren't allowed to do. And so I had my little bag — I don't bring a lunch pail — and I was carrying it through and was going upstairs when the general foreman grabbed my arm and says, "Where are you going with that bag?" I says, "I'm going upstairs." "Why? What's in the bag?" "You don't want to know." He says, "Yes I do." "It's a used Kotex pad." And he just turned around and walked away. What could I do? You've got to shut them up right off the bat or you're going to get yourself in trouble. You learn off the men what kind of attitudes to use toward supervision sometimes.

Near the beginning I had gotten blisters all over my feet from my work boots, and I wanted to go to first aid. I was refused, not knowing that I could have gone, because I didn't know what my rights were. I thought I'd better have permission and all of that. The foreman says, "No, you can't go. We need you down here." We were unloading the line at the time. Oh, my feet were just killing me! So I went on my lunch break. I ate lunch real quick and went down there to get some bandaids. And he caught me there. Well, he just gave me a blast in front of all these people. And that was embarrassing for me. I realized that there was going to be a battle between me and this man. Out there in the yard he says, "Your boots — I don't know how they could be hurting your feet. Mine aren't even worn out and I've been here for twenty years with the same pair." I said, "But the seat of your pants are pretty worn." That did it right there. I ran into more shit!

Three years later I met this man in the parking lot. Our cars met, and he tried to move me off the road. That scared me because I knew he meant business. He wanted to see me go! I tried my damndest. I slowed down. I started to speed up. No way. He had a faster car. I kept swerving over. I should have let him hit me, but I guess I was too scared.

The next day I went into the supervisor and said, "I want to talk to the manager." He says, "You can't, the manager's busy." I said, "If I don't see the manager today, I'm going to the police." About two o'clock he comes over and says, "Well, the manager's not here but the guy under him is. Will he do?" I says, "Okay, I want a meeting. I'll go and get my steward, Bruce, who's really good. Him and I were just like salt and pepper shakers. He says, "Who else do you want there?" I said, "The foreman, his supervisor and my supervisor." So we all got in there. It was Friday, about ten past two.

I had the upper hand. And I had them. For the first time in four and a half years there I finally had them. You know, when you go into a doctor's office or a lawyer's office, the phone is always ringing and they don't even say excuse me, they just answer it and talk while you're sitting there? Supervision always does that too. So I made three phone calls home to see how my kids were. And we stayed there until seven-thirty at night. On Friday. They wanted to hurry up and get home, eh? Weekend. Ah, Bruce and I were up. We were flying high, let me tell you. We felt great. Went and celebrated and had a big turkey sandwich and everything. They ended up putting a note about harassment on his record, at least it was something.

In this plant there are about twelve or thirteen women now. We started with ten and were separated to go everywhere. Three were in one department. And I worked with those women for about a year, I guess. Some of them are movie magazine readers, gossip columnists, stuff like that. They've gotta know what other people are doing, your personal life. What you do at home, who you see, who you go out with. They're more worried about that than starting a relationship with you, a friendship with you. Maybe their lives are so empty that they've got to look for something else.

The others are pretty much backers. They'll come up to me and ask, "Do you think that we can get some more heat in our dry?" I just go down and talk to supervision and say, "There's no heat upstairs. See if you can get it fixed." No big deal for me to do that. And a couple of them showed up at some of the union meetings so ... It's very slow at starting, but I think it's gonna come little by little.

I don't work with any of them now. I don't work with young men either, I work with old men, between sixty and sixty-five. I can't do them any harm and they can't do me any harm. (Laughs.) But what's really neat about it is they're coming around too. "Cath, there's three holes over by this number one conveyor. Do you think you could go and get the foreman, 'cause every time I run over with my truck, I think I'm going to dump my load."

Even though they've been there for thirty years or more, they're still afraid. I guess because they've been living like that for so long. They bitch and bitch and bitch about it. They never do anything about it. And now they can.

Not only that, they really like me working with them. They've told me it's brought new life down to the loading dock. These guys have been doing it for years and years, the same people, the same routine every day. And now we make jokes and laugh and have these little puns going back and forth. I think it's just great. I love working there with them.

I'd been working at Inco two years before I knew what a union was. I thought union had something to do with banks, like credit union. (Laughs.) I remember having some problem with work. Somebody said, "Go to the union hall and talk to Patterson." Patterson was the president. He's not much older than I am. Now we're good friends, he's told me that the first time he saw me he thought, Oh, oh, a girl in blue jeans. Here comes trouble!

I still didn't know much about unions, but there was this course that the union was putting on for a week in Hamilton, an occupational health course. It was real exciting. I don't even remember how I got on there. I think they wanted a woman to go or something. I was always interested in safety and health because of my dad's condition. He's got whitefinger syndrome — his fingers are numb and hard to use — because he was working on a drill most of his life, being a blasting captain. He got hurt one year, and I saw the pain in his face. He was paralyzed. You'd ask him a question and he'd put his hand to his ear just like an old man and ask, "What? What?" And you knew it was because of the environment he worked in. Now I'm an alternate on the safety and health committee. Have been for three years.

I started getting active, going to union meetings. I liked them until around ten o'clock at night, and then they started getting argumentative and silly. You know: "You're not in line anymore." "If you want to talk, talk to the mike." I thought, Aw, jeez, this is not a union meeting. A union meeting should be everybody that's talking about grassroots. They spend a lot of time arguing about crazy things, like donations. Who cares if ten dollars are spent on the boys' home or fifteen on this and that? That's not union.

Like I wanted to see thirty years of service and out. Because my dad worked there for forty-one years and I saw what it can do. A man like that uses up forty years of his life at Inco, then retires and dies the following year. It's just a waste, because he doesn't get piss-all for his pension after working and making all this money for this multinational company. It's a real kick in the face. So I wanted to see thirty and out.

In '78 we went on strike. I was at the union hall. A bunch of people came flying out of there saying eighty-three percent voted to reject the contract offer. And I thought, Wow, eighty-three percent. That's almost the whole thing, just about everybody. We've really got something here. There's really something deep and I've gotta know what it's about.

It was horrible at the beginning. Everybody was against us. Totally. Because they knew it would cripple the whole city. It's the only industry here. In the media we were always in the wrong. I thought, Hey, wait a minute. We don't want to get four cents over three years and a cut in our grievance procedure. All we *got* is our grievance procedure. I had a warning for taking a fifteen-minute coffee break five minutes early. I was pushing a broom at the time — it's not as though I stopped production. And every clock is different in the place. I've still got it on my record. You get one, two, three, four, then you get a day off without pay to think about it. And then you get fired. I knew how hard it was on the job, fighting through grievance procedures. I was always getting reprimanded for stupid little things.

We had cutbacks that year, massive layoffs. It was just unbelievable. Six weeks the plant was shut down in the summer and then a big strike. Who in hell had money to strike? They just put us against the wall. There was no other way out but striking. And Patterson said at the very beginning, "It's gonna be a long, hard strike." We knew that right from the beginning and we still went for it. And it was: eight and a half months.

I think what really ran the strike was a handful of people. And that became a whole family; the men and women who worked together became a big family. They started me off making sandwiches in the kitchen, putting all these egg sandwiches together for the picket line. All those eggs! There were hundreds of them, hundreds of boiled eggs. And the coffee was like you could put a knife in it and it would stand up straight. Ohhh. I went to Patterson and said, "Put me on a committee, *please*. Get me out of here." So he put me on vouchers. What we had to do was say: "John is married so he gets three dollars more for his wife. He's got two kids so he gets an order for extra money." You know?

The strike was the best thing that ever happened to me, really. It brought me out of my shell. I found out who I was, that I can do things on my own. Jeez, I got a brain. I really do. I can learn. Because I only got to grade nine I never worked with numbers, and here I was paying eleven thousand people, helping pay them with the vouchers.

Then I started giving speeches in different places, and I thought, "This is fun. I could do it all the time." But the first time was in Toronto, for a strike benefit. I don't know how I got selected. I think Patterson probably gave them my name. There were two other women, one from the wive's committee and one from the Sudbury group that supported the strike. I didn't know any of them. I'd never spoken in front of an audience in my life except for grade school. I won two little trophies for oratorical speeches in grades three and four. So my mother says, "You can probably do it since you did it when you were a kid." In front of the PTA meeting. I said, "This is a little bit different."

I was scared because I'd heard that the auditorium held five hundred or more people. And I thought, Oh my God, I can't do something like this. I couldn't write a speech. I didn't know what I was going to say, 'cause I knew if I got up there and looked at the paper, I wouldn't be able to read it. So I called Patterson and said, "Do you think that you guys can come down and listen to the speeches?"

"We're still in bargaining. We're not going to be able to make it," he said. But we left seven or eight seats just in case they could come. We were up on stage when in walked Patterson and the seven guys on the bargaining committee. Well, I'm telling you, it was like giving me a million dollars when that happened.

I couldn't wear my shoes because they had kind of high heels and my legs were wobbly. So I took them off. I went up and gave my speech and everybody was cheering and yelling. Patterson stood up and said: "I know we're on strike, but you can't be that poor not to wear shoes." This is in front of all these people. So he took his shoes off and threw them up and I'm still at the podium and I put them on, these big shoes, and say, "See Patterson, I can still fill your shoes any time." Everyone was laughing and easy and really good. It was amazing. I didn't know that people were enthusiastic about strikes or knew what was going on. Here we were up in Sudbury. Nobody knew Sudbury until the strike, and now everybody knew Sudbury. I just loved it.

And plant-gating. Everybody would go down on a bus somewhere and stay in a hotel that's paid for by the union that asks you to go. And you stand outside the gates and when the guys or women come off work, they put money in your pot. Not just steelworkers. We went to General Motors. We went to Hamilton, brought back ten thousand dollars.

It was wonderful. The togetherness. Times between, when we weren't out at the gate, everyone would pick one room and fifteen, twenty, thirty people would be in this one room. And there would be guitars and singing and drinking. (Laughs.) We went lots of places, mostly down south: St. Catharines, Windsor, Oshawa.

We didn't have any hospitalization or drug coverage during the strike. It's really hard when a woman says, "My baby is diabetic and I need insulin and we don't have any money." We would look at them and say, "I'll get you some." (Laughs.) That's your attitude. And you just go out and get it.

During the strike the wives of workers got together. I liked that these women were interested in what their husbands were doing. I went to a meeting about bargaining, and these women were at the door giving out pamphlets saying: "Come to the bean supper." A bean supper? What the hell are they making a bean supper for?

So I grabbed a pamphlet and was about to go in, when this man behind me says to one of the women, "What are you doing here? You have no business at this union hall." I turned around and said, "Of course they have. They're on strike just like their husbands are on strike. They're going to have to go through a lot, too." So the woman said, "Thank you. Why don't you come to one of our meetings?" So I went. And it was exciting! All these women. Really huffing and puffing. Now *this* was a union meeting. This is where it was happening. They just came out of the woodwork. From their salt, pepper and spice atmosphere, children's diapers, the whole works, to this — radical women. It was unbelievable. There were about forty, I guess. More than a membership meeting almost. "Jeez, can I come back? This is really interesting." They said, "Sure.'"

When I came back the second time, the filmers came in. They wanted to make a movie about the strike, the wives. So I left. I was waiting outside. Someone came out. "Cathy, you are now part of our group. You can come in while they're filming." Holy jeez, eh? I felt good about the women.

Because I've hung around men most of my life. Baseball, hockey, street games, stuff like that. Always hanging around with my brothers. My sisters and I never really hung around together. I was interested in what men were brought up for. I guess I was very rebellious. My mother would say, "Cathy and Sandra, do the dishes." I would lock myself up in the bathroom until the dishes were done, because my brothers were playing outside and I didn't think it was fair.

But one night with the wives and I felt really comfortable. They were really neat people. I felt then that I was part of the group. Sure, it was divided in half like any other group. There was the right wing and the left wing. And of course I was in the left wing. (Laughs.) It was really great to see these women active and coming out. It was like the inner person, the inner them that they couldn't always let out. And when I saw them coming out of their shells, it was so good. They started accepting me, too. They asked me to speak at one of their meetings about safety and health, as well as a little bit about bargaining. I explained what the grievance procedures were, stuff like that that they didn't know because they hadn't been involved before.

It was Christmas. What were we going to do about presents for the kids? The wives said we'd try to get together as many toys as possible. We'd get these old puzzles, and pieces would be missing. "Forget it. We can't use this." Washing old dolls that had crayon marks on them. We bagged them, all these old toys. And then, just like Christmas was supposed to be, it was like a miracle. Truckloads and truckloads of brand new toys came in. The wives stayed up all night bagging them. Hockey sticks, skates, you name it. All the unions, but mostly Hamilton and others down south, had sent them. Fantastic. Toys piled right to the ceiling of the union hall. Thousands. Ten thousand children got toys. Unbelievable. And it was a great day because it was like being Santa Claus. "Here you go, take this, take that. Take it all." Parents and kids came. They had a Santa Claus, a few Santa Clauses. Everybody took their turn dressing up. I said, "Wouldn't want a female Santa Claus?" (Laughs.) They wouldn't go for that. It was great anyway.

But towards the end of the strike the enthusiasm died. There was just hate. And all this deceiving stuff, like redbaiting going on inside the union. It was splitting up all over the place. So the wives decided to put on a play. Because we couldn't go to Toronto to the Inco shareholders' meeting, we decided to hold something up here.

It took us three days to put together. That's all the time we had. In this play, we decided to bring these shareholders to court and lay charges against them. Everybody charged them with something. Bruce charged them with violating safety and health. I charged them with negligence. Another charged them with murder because her uncle had been killed, died of cancer. There was about six of us who charged them with something.

We got money together to fly Patterson back from Toronto where he was bargaining, to say what he charged Inco with: bargaining in bad faith. He came after five o'clock after they finished bargaining for the day, came all the way up to Sudbury, did that and went back on the eleven o'clock flight.

All the wives were dressed up. One was perfect. She had on this tuxedo that she had got from somebody and she had a pipe in her mouth. We had masks out of plaster of Paris and painted them all. We had this other woman dressed up in this little doll outfit, walking around serving the shareholders while they were in court. So the atmosphere would look like they've got it made. The audience was the jury. At the end we asked, "Is Inco guilty or not guilty?" The whole audience shouted, "Guilty, guilty, guilty! Off with their heads!" And out came this security guard with this axe made of tinfoil.

The newspaper was there and said we were too violent. (Laughs.) We didn't think anything was wrong. It was just a play.

We went back June 3, 1979. I went back to the anode. It was a different type of atmosphere. The guys were so supportive it was unbelievable. They knew what I had done during the strike. I wasn't expecting anything, but I got something out of it, you know? The guys said, "Jeez, I seen you on TV." Or, "I read your article." I was shocked. "You care about what I do?" Even the foremen and the supervisors stayed away from me. They didn't bother me like they did before. No following me to the washroom. So I find it totally different now. Even myself, I've changed a lot.

During the strike I went through my separation. I was married for eight years, and I just realized that this was not what I wanted anymore.

I was always having to explain at home who I talked to, why I talked to them, what I talked about. And then I'd get shit for something I'd said that afternoon at the coffee shop or something. And it was happening at work the same way and I just couldn't take it anymore.

He was threatened by my working with a bunch of men, I guess. I never saw it. I just never saw it. "You know you can trust me." It didn't make any sense to me to fool around. But I guess he was threatened. I made more money, but I don't think that mattered because it paid the bills. But I think the whole fact of my being independent probably scared him a lot.

I had always been his family, tagging along, looking after the kids at the baseball game, the hockey games that he and his brother played in. It was always the same people. I thought, "This is a drag, I'm boxed in. I haven't any place to breathe or even to look sideways without getting shit for it." If we'd stop for a beer after a baseball game and somebody wasn't in a union, they'd start in. Then I'd say something: "That's not right; this is how it is." At home, my husband would say, "You don't have to talk like that."

But I did have to. And I realized I wasn't "his wife" anymore. We were two totally different people. We weren't on the same level anymore. The strike made it a lot worse.

But I had been contemplating separation for over two years already. Going through marriage counsellors, trying to save this thing we had. You can never go back. You've always got to go ahead. And I found out it was gone. The love wasn't there.

And then it became dislike. It was a waste, such a waste of energy. It came to the point where we'd sit for two or three months at a time and never even say, "Pass the salt." And I'm a talker. I can't handle that. I can't handle quietness.

I think it was coming because a lot of bullshit was being thrown at me personally. Like a lot of things at work, a lot of things from the strike, a lot of things from home and the kids. It happened all at once and I thought, "Cathy, get off your ass and leave. You're out of step. You've stopped. You've gotta get moving or you're not going anywhere." And I did.

I thought for sure I would have a nervous breakdown. But when I went to the doctor's, he said, "Now, you're too stubborn to have a breakdown. Your body will give out first." Which was true. For a year I was in pain all the time. I went in for an operation, then another one. It was scary. But the back-up from the guys at work and the friends I met during the strike and my sisters, the wives, made it so much better.

I would be lying there chopped up into pieces and they would be saying, "You look like you were in a fight and lost." "What a thing to hear when you wake up. Thanks." (Laughs.) It doesn't matter. They're there to see you, the inside. Your body's just to get around in anyways. (Laughs.)

When I started at Inco my dad was totally displeased with me. It was no place for his little girl. I used to be called "little one." It was no place for "little one" to work. I was nineteen and short. Very tiny. I love it. I've talked to armpits all my life. (Laughs.) He was totally displeased with me. But over the years he's been trying to fight the Compensation Board about his back injury and his hands. And now he talks to *me* about it. He calls me and talks to me about the letters he got from Compensation.

And now, when I go over for supper, I always sit at the head of the table and he sits at the other end of the table. And the family sits on the side. Because that's the way it is. I am equal with my father. And he respects me because of it. He won't really come out and say it, but he doesn't have to.

Our whole family is wonderful to me. I can call my mom and say, "Mom, I want to go to Halifax. Will you babysit for me?" "Sure, I'll be right over." Anything. All you got to do is ask. I don't know what she really thinks about unions and stuff. But I know she supports me. She knows what I'm like. And she knows it doesn't matter what she says, I'm going to do it anyway. (Laughs.)

I've always been this way. My daughter's exactly the same way. If it doesn't go your way, it doesn't go any way. You know it's not being selfish. It's being determined.

During the strike I found out there was a whole different world of friends out there that I had never experienced before. Women with the same problems, women that were twenty-three, going through the changes from being a child, really, to becoming a woman. Feeling that change with everybody, and going through it. I don't even need ice cream anymore. (Laughs.) I don't eat candy anymore. These women that I hung around with during the strike are my best friends now.

Arja was one of the women. Her husband, Austin, works in the anode as a craneman. Crane person? Crane *operator!* (Laughs.) And the relationship Arja and I have is so good that nothing could possibly break it. We hunt and fish together. Then if I decide to go with her husband, fishing or camping, it's all right. No big deal. He's just a person. I'm not looking at him as a sex object, or vice versa.

If I was going to stay at Inco all my life, I'd want to get a job where at the end of a shift I could say, "Well, I done good today." I liked that when I was casting fine shapes. The copper is much purer there and is cast in special shapes that different companies use. I cast wire bars that weighed 250 to 300 pounds and were ninety-nine percent pure. I worked hard, and when I got a good product out and didn't get any scrap left, I liked it. I felt good. I thought, jeez, I've done a whole three thousand bars today and I only got two scrap (rejects). I'd like it if the company would come out and say, "You did a good job today." And you *know* you did a good job. But they don't appreciate what we're doing.

Personally, I want to pay off my house. In the meantime I've got to learn everything I can learn. Doesn't matter what it is. I'm learning now about my truck — tune-ups, tire changes, brakeshoes — so I don't have to get on the phone and ask, "George, will you come over and fix my car for me?" I don't want to do that. I want to be able to say, "Well, I've got to go out and change my antifreeze. I've got to mow my lawn and clean up my yard, because I don't want anybody else doing it for me."

And I would like to go back to school, maybe take a mechanics course. Learn some math. Go back and take math and an English course. From then on, either working with animals or working with cars.

I'm at the point in my life where I can say, Whatever I want, I can get. I feel really good about that. Self-reliance and self-confidence. Sometimes *over*-self-confidence. (Laughs.) But I know that I can do it. I can do anything.

Inco laid off thousands of workers in 1981 and 1982. Fortunately, Cathy had enough seniority to keep her job. She is back working on the cast in the copper refinery and is still active in the union.

Steelworkers Jeannette Easson, Debbie Field
and Joanne Santucci at the Steel Company of Canada (Stelco),
Hamilton, Ontario

WORKING STEEL

JEANNETTE   EASSON

DEBBIE   FIELD
&
JOANNE   SANTUCCI

We MET IN JEANNETTE's *living room on a muggy summer afternoon in 1981, shortly after the Steelworkers' Local 1005 had struck Stelco, a strike which was to last four months. The electricity was off and Jeannette was waiting for a repairman. In the meantime she connected up the tape recorder with extension cords to a plug in her neighbour's house, then apologized to us for the lack of cold beer. We drank it warm.*

The three women were obviously good friends, warm and comfortable with each other. Jeannette, in her late thirties and a single mothers of three boys, spun out long, enthusiastic stories of her experiences. Debbie, who had recently quit her job at Stelco, spoke in rapid, usually articulate bursts. Joanne was quiet at the beginning but later got very funny, mugging and gesturing expressively to punctuate her remarks.

The women were in high spirits, partly because of enthusiasm for the strike itself, partly because of a reprieve from shiftwork. They talked for hours about working at Stelco, reminding each other of old stories, encouraging each other, laughing, interrupting and freely disagreeing without rancour.

JEANNETTE: The first time I applied at Stelco, I was just out of grade thirteen. I was eighteen years old, just newly married. That was in 1962, about the last year Stelco hired a woman until 1980. I didn't get the job.

This time, 1979, I had just gone through a divorce and was enrolled in a Manpower welding course. I saw this article in the paper, Cec Taylor (president of Local 1005) saying that Stelco had hired a female doctor. Saying some of the guys were uptight about getting examined by a female doctor, but wasn't it nice that Stelco had hired a woman. And wasn't it strange that Stelco hadn't hired a woman for a production job in almost twenty years, and unless the women in the Hamilton area complained, there was nothing that could be done.

DEBBIE: He said that if there were any women who wanted jobs at Stelco, they should contact him. So about ten women called him. Jeannette was one of them and I was one.

I was working as the equal opportunities co-ordinator for OPSEU (the Ontario Public Service Employees' Union) and was frustrated by how little I was able to do in that position, because the unequal wages of men and women in the union continued to expand. I couldn't see how that was going to change.

I was also very frustrated as a staffer in a union because I felt that I couldn't do anything *real*. I wanted to do something myself. I didn't want to be advising other people to do things. And I was very angry about the way union staffs don't represent the members. I wanted to do something on the ground in that way.

Second, I was a member of a left group that thought the best way to build socialist activity in unions was to have their members go into industrial workplaces. So I came to Hamilton as part of a group of ten or fifteen people of similar persuasion. I'm no longer a member of that group, and I see some real problems with that strategy now.

A third reason was more personal. I had always been relatively unathletic and not very good at a lot of physical stuff, so I was romantically excited by the possibility of being able to do a manual job, being able to show that I could do it, not to have to work with my head all the time but with my hands. To actually see what it's like.

JEANNETTE: We applied for jobs. We were never actually turned down, but female applications just got thrown in the bottom drawer and never looked at.

DEBBIE: You'd go in and they'd look at you as if you were out of your mind. They'd try to give you an application for the office. One woman had the experience of seeing her application go into this special drawer. She looked at the pile — which she said was about eight hundred — and saw they were all women's names.

The union figured out that ten percent of all applicants to Stelco over the years had been women. I don't know where they got this figure or even if it's true. (Laughter.) I think it was an approximation which got to be truth and then we got stuck with it, 'cause we demanded they hire women in proportion to the applications.

JEANNETTE: We decided to form a committee to pressure Stelco to hire some women. We called it "Women into Stelco." We knew that if you just said "Women into Industry," you would not get support, but if you said "Women into Stelco," everybody else except Stelco would say, "Hey, we'll go along with that." (Laughter.)

We put the "back" in later — "Women Back into Stelco" — over Chinese food across the road. That was to advertise the fact that women used to be there. Even women in the community would say, "What woman would *want* to work at Stelco?" Well, "Back into Stelco" signified that there *were* women in there once. Women had been pushed out of jobs at Stelco since the war, and now we wanted back in.

We decided collectively that the best way to get at Stelco would be by charging them through the Human Rights Commission. It wouldn't cost us a lawyer, it would be all very legal, and it would look good to the public.

We set up an appointment with a Human Rights officer. She gave us a rundown on what would take place if we did charge with the commission. We discussed it among ourselves, told her we'd like to charge Stelco with discrimination against women in hiring, and to put on a public campaign. We went from there — set up appointments to lay charges at the Human Rights office and to have a press conference the day after that.

Human Rights has the tradition of being non-public — they won't go public with any of their information or findings. But we thought the best way we could win the thing was to put on a massive public advertising campaign, get the support and endorsation of all the unions. And we wouldn't have won without a public campaign. It's as simple as that.

DEBBIE: Three days after our first press conference, Stelco tried to take the heat off themselves by hiring two women. One of them quit the first day. That was a real drag. There was a lot of bad publicity about that. The woman had been a crane operator at Dofasco, the other big steel company in town. She thought she'd be able to operate a crane right away. Well, at Stelco you have to have seniority to be on a crane.

JOANNE: She had to slap this grease on the rolls, right? She said, "No, no. I want to work up there." (Gesturing. Laughs.) In ten years you might work up there, right? "Well, I want to work up there." (Laughter.) "I don't want to slap grease on rolls." So they said, "I'm sorry, toots. Grab a pail or hit the road." She hit the road.

DEBBIE: Stelco was very stupid about us all along. Dofasco had been hiring women as crane operators for years. This keeps women separated from everybody else, up there in their own little cab, and it's not really like getting women in there. But they can say, and for years have said, "We don't discriminate."

But Stelco's attitude was, "No fucking way we're going to let women work here." If they'd been smart, they could have scooped us — hired some women before we managed to get a press conference. But they didn't. It was really stupid from their point of view.

I think we made a lot of mistakes, but one thing that wasn't a mistake was setting up the committee. It was fantastic. In these situations, all the pressures on you are to do less, to shut up and be quieter. The Human Rights Commission was saying, "No, no, no. Be quiet. Wait. Just relax. Let us do it." The union at Stelco was also sort of saying, "We'll handle it. Let us do it in our way."

But the strength of the campaign was that we did everything ourselves. We had this committee where the decisions were made. Most of the committee were not women who actually wanted to work at Stelco. One of the crucial people, for instance, was a white-collar worker, a clerk-typist working at the Red Cross. She wasn't interested in working at Stelco, but she really saw the importance of the campaign, and we couldn't have done it without her. So we had women like that in the committee, women who supported the women's movement.

There were people who were feminists, leftists, but there were people who weren't too. There were five of us who laid the human rights complaints, five ringleaders. Two of us, another woman and myself, were organized leftists. Jeannette is a progressive, pro-union type person but is not in any political group. And the other two women had no political goals at all. So it was sort of half and half. We had a lot of energy and a lot of skills.

We met every single week. We met too much, in fact. We'd meet and talk and figure stuff out and leaflet, send letters. We sent letters to all the unions in Hamilton. That was really important, because we got support from these one hundred percent male locals.

We were in the newspapers about once a week I think, for about two and a half months. We were on radio and on television. We had a demonstration of about twenty people one day in a snowstorm in December, in front of the Stelco towers.

We had arguments and differences, but it was mostly fun. We would always go drinking after a meeting. There was a nice feeling of being part of a collective that was doing something.

JEANNETTE: There were fellas on the committee too, but it was like — what do you say — a sorority? Everybody together.

DEBBIE: Jeannette and I worked basically full-time on it for three months. She and I were both unemployed. She was eating ravioli (laughter) here with her kids and not making any money, and I was on unemployment, waiting to get into a Manpower course, a machine shop course at Mohawk College. So she and I would go down to the union hall and xerox and gestetner and do all that kind of stuff.

JEANNETTE: We were very aware that as long as the campaign looked good for Local 1005's executive, then they would let us operate, they'd back us. We could use the printing room, the typewriters, whatever we wanted. But we had to be careful not to offend them, to keep them happy so they'd continue to support us.

Issues like this die fast. You can only say "Women Charge Stelco" once in the paper and then it's old news. But we had to keep going and going, press conferences and all that. We had to keep involving the executive; that way we could get to use the rooms for meetings; that way 1005 could say, "Hey, we're still after this women's issue."

DEBBIE: This should be said. If it hadn't been for Cec Taylor, all this wouldn't have happened. He is a feminist of a kind, in his own way. He always tells us about how his mom was a machinist during the war, and he had to wash dishes and take care of his brother and all that.

But he's also very shrewd politically, and he saw, in a way that a lot of less shrewd union guys didn't see, that this would go somewhere. He knew that we would work, and we really did, and we got him a tremendous amount of credibility for it. But it was a hard issue. He stuck his neck out a bit. Because now, a year later, not all the guys at Stelco want women to work there.

We made the mistake of not involving enough other people. We were never able to break out of the kind of public relations campaign we had built in the beginning. Jeannette had been in real estate and had a great understanding of leaflets. I'd worked for a union, and a couple of us had been in left groups, so we could always give press conferences. We had good relations with the *Spectator:* they'd write what we'd say. But what we didn't know how to do was reach the women out there, like Joanne Santucci here, who were actually looking for the jobs.

We had ideas about this. We were going to do a mass application-in. We were going to get a thousand women to all go down and apply at the same time. We were going to go to the high schools. We had all these ideas, but we were never able to carry them out. And it made us weaker.

We were really a small committee — fifteen to twenty people most of the time — even though we had people supporting us. But those people were't *there*. It means to this day that women in that plant don't know each other. Because we never met before.

JOANNE: I was thinking, though, if you had done that, reached us directly somehow, and women like myself found out what you guys were really into, the political stuff, you might have really alienated yourselves.

We were just going in there because we had to put food on the table and we needed a job. Better Stelco than a pizza joint, you know?

It's scary when you hear "commie." I mean, I'm a nice Italian Catholic girl, you know what I mean? (Laughter.) If someone says "commie" to me, it's like leprosy, you know? (Laughter.)

When I first started working at Stelco, someone mentioned the woman who works in the machine shop. So I wanted to meet her, 'cause I'm a libber from way back, right?

So my dad takes me aside for a father-daughter talk, which I've never really had with him before. My father is a foreman at Stelco, so it's not really a father-daughter talk; it's a foreman-employee talk. (Gales of laughter.) But he's disguising it very well. He pulls me aside and he says, "Joanne," he looks around (peering furtively), "her underwear is *red*!" So I sit there. And I'm thinking, "Well, maybe she had her period that day." (Laughter.) I say, "Dad, how do you know what colour her underwear is?" And he says, "It's just like Cec Taylor and all those other jerks." I still don't understand. "I'll explain it to you one more way." He goes, "You fly with the ducks, people think you're a duck." (Laughter.) You fly with the ducks — what the hell does that mean? And then he finally comes out and says, "Commies, commies, Joanne. They're all commies." So I'm walking around, "His underwear is red," you know? Wishing they wore white pants so I could tell.

Seriously, though, it kind of scared me. I went to meetings and one woman was going wild: "We've got to stick together."

You had to tell her to hold it down a couple of times, Debbie, remember? Get back to the issue, right? And I'm sitting there going, "Ducks, eh?" (Laughter.)

DEBBIE: There was a lot of talk in the union too that we were all commies. It's a complicated thing to sort out. You don't want to scare people away, because obviously most people in society are not communists or feminists or anything, but on the other hand you don't want to have to pretend and lie about what you are. I am a socialist, and because I'm a socialist I work harder on these sorts of things than if I wasn't politically committed.

Anyway, for months we kept on doing our usual stuff, but we were losing steam. No one was getting hired. So we came up with the idea that International Women's Day, March 8, 1980, would be a big Women Back into Stelco effort. And we organized a great rally. I think it was one of the best political rallies ever held in Hamilton.

JEANNETTE: There was a TV program and afternoon talk show the week before it, and the big rally was on a Saturday. We were kind of uptight about it; everybody was being very negative. And it was a tremendous success. We had to bring in more chairs. We had women saying, "Where do I sign up? Where do I sign up?" We had folk singers, a bar, everything. We had women down from Inco in Sudbury, some of the first women who were in the plant; we had striking Bell workers, which was a hot issue at that time; we had the Radio Shack strikers. We had Cec Taylor, of course. (Laughs.) It was really just a tremendous success. Rather than just a celebration it turned out to be a bloody rally. Three hundred people signing up. "Where do I join for Women Back into Stelco?"

DEBBIE: Two weeks later Human Rights says Stelco is prepared to talk. It gave us a nice feeling. When I am a hundred years old, I will remember that we were capable of making Stelco jump to — not only our demands, but our pace, you know? It really infuriated them that they were unable to take away the initiative.

We wanted to go in to be interviewed together, the five of us. Stelco said, "No way." They kept arguing that we were five individual cases, that if we were hired or not had nothing to do with the fact that we were women. But Human Rights found out that, let's say for the month of October alone, there were twenty-five or thirty people hired with less experience than even myself, who had the least industrial experience among us. In that way the Human Rights Commission was very useful, because they subpoenaed all those applications.

And so we said, "We're not going in." All week long we had these midnight telephone conversations with the Human Rights Officer. She'd say, "Well, I called Stelco and they won't talk to all five of you together. If you want to call it off..." I'd say, "But we're scared; we don't want to go in alone." Finally we agreed. And in fact it was very scary. It would have been much better had we not gone in alone.

They took the woman who had been the least active in the campaign first. She went in and came out with a job, and that was it. The second one in was the youngest woman of us, about nineteen, and she'd been really behind us the whole way, but she hadn't talked to the press a lot. So they gave her a job, no problem. Gave her a job at the tin mill. There were some other women there left over from the war. It was the nicest place a woman could get a job in Stelco.

The third woman in got a bit of a hard time, but they gave her a job as an apprentice. She didn't want to apprentice. She had been a machinist at another factory. But they made her take it. And we were very timid. We were prepared to take anything.

I went in next and they said, "Sorry." We were really surprised. Human Rights was really surprised. They thought all this was going to go fine. But they said, "We don't hire men with your education. They don't last." So we told them I was enrolled in a course in a machine shop, and eventually they said okay. They put me in coke ovens, one of the worst parts of the plant.

Then Jeannette went in and all hell broke out.

JEANNETTE: I was the last one to be called in. They had me labelled. I'm the spokeswoman; they're going to break me. They told me if I had the inclination to put in another application, they just might possibly look at it.

A week later I got called for an interview. By coincidence, my whole speech from the rally was printed in *Steel Shots,* the union paper, which hit the plant gate that day. In it I made a joke about the blast furnace.

JOANNE: (Laughing.) Bad move, eh?

JEANNETTE: This is true. What I said in the speech was, they say women can't handle the heavier jobs at Stelco, like the blast furnaces, but we know that women handled those jobs in the days that the company was less mechanized. I said my aunt worked in the blast furnaces thirty-five years ago. I'd certainly like a chance to take on my aunt's old job.

JOANNE: And Debbie would be dying to get into the coke ovens. (Laughs.)

JEANNETTE: I went in for the interview. He brings me a coffee. And then he slams the door. "We know who you are." He's got the file with all the different newspaper clippings from our whole campaign in front of him. "Do you realize you embarrassed Stelco? Are you in this for political reasons? Is it your intention to be a disruptive force if Stelco should offer you a job? Answer me!" He went into this over and over. And all the time I'm thinking, "He has to hire me. If I can last this tongue-lashing, I've got a job." Anyway, he finished up and he's offering me . . . the blast furnaces.

I think they worked out our placement very carefully, not just haphazardly. The woman they put in an apprenticeship is on the line for five years. It's like five years' probation, so she won't step out of line. Debbie, who's very active, very health and safety conscious, they put in coke ovens, where they weed out people like her. They only put non-active people in there. They put Debbie where it would be very frustrating for her, as well as being very harmful to her as a woman wanting to have a family, or whatever. It's one of the unhealthiest places in the plant.

They put me in blast furnaces really to get even with me. They put me in the dirtiest place. Guys falling over. I think the main thing I've done in there is get a few things cleaned up.

Joanne was hired six months later.

JOANNE: Everything I've ever done has always been a hundred guys and me, or fifty guys and me. I've always gone against the grain of everything, right? It just happened that way. My interests lie differently, right? And that's how I got into it. I was working at Shoprite. I said, "Piss on this, man. I'm going down to Stelco." My dad says to me, "Don't go and apply there." I goes, "Dad, I'm going there and apply. So just forget it."

So I went down there with a friend of mine, a guy. He got an application and I got an application. He got an interview two days later. I waited almost two weeks for an interview. This was after they had already hired women. I was really pissed off. So he got in and I was all depressed.

Then I got sick. I had to go to the hospital. So here I am, on my bed, intravenous going and everything, and I get this call. The nurse says, "Call your sister, it's an emergency." Here I am with an intravenous hanging out of my arm and I've got to call home for an emergency! (Laughs.) I call home. My sister says, "Stelco called. They want you to come for an interview." I went, "Ohhhh." (Laughter.) So I grabbed this intravenous bottle, jumped out of bed, ran all the way down the hall to this lady's semi-private room where she had a phone. So I call them up, right? This woman says, "Can you come in for an interview day after tomorrow?" I'm supposed to be in hospital another week. So I say, "Yeah, no problem." She goes, "Accompanying the interview, you have to go for a medical. Any medical problems?" And there I am. (Laughter.) I say, "No problems at all. I'll be there."

And I went down. The interview was pretty funny. "Does your father know you're applying here?" So what am I doing, something illegal? And then he went off on a whole bunch of tangents. He never did ask me anything about Stelco. I told him I worked in about five construction companies out west. (Laughter.) I said I worked in about four factories in Hamilton. I did wonderful. (Laughter.) They hired me.

"Your job is labourer." Okay, I'll get the broom. No problem. Groomed for this type of work.

I started in the rolling mill, where they roll the steel out in sheets. When I first walked into this mill I was horrified. I just couldn't believe it. There were sirens going everywhere. The cranes, I don't know how many there were, but one was always flying over my head with a load.

The guy who showed me around was a complete dink, trying to intimidate me by taking me into the worst part of the plant, without warning me about the dangers, and laughing at me when I jumped at sudden noises.

Walking through the mill, it was weird. It felt like you had three noses and two heads or something. You'd walk down the mill and all of a sudden this head would pop out of nowhere and pop right back, right? (Laughs.) "Like, wow, a broad!" Staring constantly.

DEBBIE: That was one thing that used to drive me nuts. I was a general labourer, so the first few months I shovelled coal, coke mostly. Coke is coal that has already been cooked, little lumps. And we would clean up the tracks. It reminded me of those movies about prison gangs. We would go out with our crew boss following us and we'd shovel the coke into wheelbarrows and move it off the track and dump it somewhere else.

We'd go out there, and there's like ten males, two women, and we're shovelling, and sometimes you'd be trying to shovel through about two feet of coke off a track. It's a little hard to get your shovel in, and it takes a while to really know how to do it. And you'd look up and there'd be about twenty guys lookin' like they'd never seen a shovel, never seen a human being in their life before, just laughing and pointing and staring.

One day there was this women student who was having real trouble learning how to do this, and the guys were just up there laughing. I finally shouted, "Fuck off. Go away. Leave us alone." And everybody thought, Aw, she's so sensitive.

I think things have changed now, but the first time I used the wheelbarrow, there was like a hundred guys standing there watching me. Where they came from, I don't know. Of course, once I dumped the wheelbarrow and they just loved that!

JEANNETTE: When I started, every guy and his brother was coming up to me as if I was *the* woman. This is what woman is, me. And "Why are you here? Why is this?" Asking me all kinds of questions. They looked at me as if every woman that was ever employed at Stelco was going to be five-foot-one with black curly hair and have a big mouth. I had to point out that, "No, there are five women. I'm loud. I talk a lot. There are very introverted women. There are tall women. I'm short. I'm fat. There are skinny women. There are all kinds of women. I'm only *one*."

Later on, as more women were hired, we did run the gamut in women, although there's been only a half dozen ever hired in the blast furnaces. There hasn't been a woman hired in the blast furnaces for over a year now. But the guys were full of questions.

I started my first day on an electric car. I walk on the car and the guy who's to train me, I guess he didn't realize it was a female coming. He's a quiet guy, kind of embarrassed. He says, "Holy Christ. Now I can't piss on the ore." (Laughs.) 'Cause when you're on the train you're on there an hour at least, sometimes two. If you've gotta go, the guys just piss into the ore. And I said, "What in hell am *I* goin' to do? Sit on the edge of the train and hang over?" (Laughs.)

We had to clean up slag off the tracks, hot metal that had spilled off. You have to put hooks into it, get a bulldozer to pull it up, pry it up. The work's kind of heavy, but not too hard. They used to pack the wheelbarrows, these construction wheelbarrows, with heavy metal chunks, and dirt and scrap off the ground. They would pack the wheelbarrow full, mound it up, pack it down with their shovels, fuller and fuller, until it's falling off. "Allright, now. Try and push that!" They did this little game, everybody did it to each other. It wasn't just with me. But they sort of expected *me* not to be able to do it. It's kind of a joke. I was raised on a farm. I've pushed wheelbarrows before.

JOANNE: I didn't bend over for about two weeks. You were so conscious that if you bent over they'd be just waiting. Oh fuck, I couldn't stand it. And all these broads in town saying, "Oh, you must *love* the attention!" (Laughter.) At first, I got blamed for crowds. It was my fault. As if I had a magnet and was zicking everybody out all around me, right? (Laughter.) Like, one day I was in this pulpit, like an operator's booth. I went in to ask a couple of questions, find out what's going on. The next thing you know another guy comes in, a couple millwrights come in, an electrician comes in, right? And there's this little pulpit, everybody stuffed in, and they're all smoking, and all of a sudden you hear over the PA system: "All you guys get the *fuck* out of there!" I get called up to the foreman's office, and it's my fault because I'm causing crowds, right?

I thought the guys were harassing me at first because they were always around me, constantly eyeing me. So I'd go to the foreman, and he'd say, "Look, you're new; you're a novice here. They're just thrilled that you're here." Thrilled is not the word.

And so I'd run to the foreman. But what happened in the end was that it all went in reverse. The guys ended up being my protectors and the foremen ended up sticking it to me. All the time.

DEBBIE: It wasn't that way all the time. In the coke ovens, and I've heard this from people in other mills, sometimes the foreman would be quite reasonable, and in fact he would be a problem in reverse. Because some of the foremen are very chauvinist. They would try to give the women softer jobs. In our area there was this one job, truckloader, which is very boring but a very soft job. You sit in this booth. And all the guys hated it because it was so boring. But the women actually liked it a lot because it was the easiest job there. And they would always get the women students to do that job. I think the foreman thought that he was being a nice guy. But in fact it was worse for the women because the guys would go nuts at any special treatment. We *didn't* always get easy jobs, just this one easy job this one foreman would give us.

JEANNETTE: All the foremen were really uptight about the women working there. They don't want their wives to work. My ex-husband was a Stelco foreman. For eighteen years of marriage to him I could cut an acre of grass in the back lawn, but I couldn't go and cut this little strip in front, five feet wide, because the neighbours would see his wife working, and Stelco foremen don't have their wives working. They're earning enough that their wives don't have to work. They take pride in their wives not working.

JOANNE: The foreman was constantly calling me to the office. "If you don't think you can do it, just let me know." I'd go, "I can do it. Anything you've got. Give it to me."

DEBBIE: The work was not that hard. That's one of the reasons that women can survive the jobs. We never had any trouble with the work. But conditions are awful. That has to be made absolutely clear. It is a terrible, dehumanizing, awful place to work. And dirty, dirty, dirty. Everywhere. It really grinds on you. Grinds on the guys too. And it doesn't have to be that way. It could be changed. For example, the shifts. They have some of the worst shifts in the world. Three rotating shifts, never the same days off for most people, weekends once every three months. You don't even get a vacation after the first year. You want to go to a party on Saturday night, they give you a hassle.

JEANNETTE: No freedom.

DEBBIE: No freedom at all. It's ridiculous, very badly organized. The rules are very authoritarian. We couldn't go back to the lunchroom, even in the pouring rain, during our breaks. We had to take our coffee break right on the tracks.

After a while I went to the ovens, for which you need a little more seniority. There I did the very, very deadly jobs. There are a lot of jobs that service the ovens when the coke is cooking. That involves running through gas and turning levers on and off and sweeping excess coal and coke into holes and stuff. Again, the work was relatively simple, physically. I got better muscles, and I got in good shape and felt really good to be running around and stuff. There were a few jobs that were tough physically. I couldn't shovel as well as some guys. But then again I'm not as strong as Joanne and Jeannette are. I'm probably one of the weaker women who started there. And there were some who were worse than me. (Laughs.)

JOANNE: There was one woman. Weighs about ninety pounds. The size of my leg. (Laughs.)

DEBBIE: Stelco definitely hired some women who weren't very strong. I think they did that on purpose.

JEANNETTE: There are guys too who cannot lift or anything. But none of the jobs are really physically demanding for a long period.

DEBBIE: On the other hand, I think it's important that we not romanticize our strength and say we're exactly the same as guys. Or that all women are as good as all guys are at the stuff. 'Cause that's not true. The point is, there are lots of women who *are* as good, and they should be given a chance.

One of the jobs that we had to do is called lidsman — lidsperson, they began to call it while I was there. (Laughter.) And it's the worst, the highest cancer rate of any job at Stelco, because when coal is cooked in these big ovens and turned to coke, all these poisonous gases flow out of it. Stelco could clean it up, but they haven't. They could create better seals that wouldn't leak, and things like that. There are these standpipes which let air into the ovens. And there's a row of tar which accumulates on top of the standpipe. And you have to crack this cap open. You have to grab onto this lever, and pull it open. And the cap weighs maybe *sixty pounds.* Now, if everything's fine and there's no tar on the bottom, then most people could do it. Most women could do it. You just go out and crack it and then you open it. But Stelco doesn't keep it clean. It's a management problem. I mean, it's workers who have to *do* it, but they're not assigned to do it.

So I went out there one day, and about every tenth one I couldn't open. You could take a bar and hit it and hit it and hit it. And one big guy once threw his back out doing that.

So I was working with a guy who was a bit union conscious, and he said, "Let's not open them. Let's just leave them." And of course, they came up and started screaming and hollering and assumed immediately that it was all mine that hadn't been opened. But his hadn't been opened either. Now, this big two-hundred-pound foreman came out, walked up to all these things and just cracked them, right? So it's true that a guy who's really strong could've done them in a way that I couldn't. But my argument was that if they were kept clean, there wasn't a job I couldn't do there. But in crisis situations where things are really falling apart, where Stelco's not doing their job of maintenance, it was true, there were some jobs I couldn't do as well as most of the guys could.

JOANNE: I think I shocked them a few times. Once they had me pick up these stop blocks. They're heavy metal blocks they move along the track to hold the train from rolling. They're sixty-five, seventy-five pounds each. I picked one up, almost broke my back. I was weight-lifting a lot then, so I went back to the basics, how to pick things up. I was walking all bent over. So the only logical thing to do was to pick two up, one in each hand. That would even me up. So I did it. It was killing me to do it, but it would kill me more just to pick one up. The guys were walking by going, "My God!"

All the old guys took to me the most. They made me tea, they brought me stuff. "My wife made me these cookies. How would you like one?" I've got a good sense of humour and I really took every guy I met as an individual. "What's your wife's name?" I'd remember their wives. I'd remember their kids' names. So the next time they'd say, "Oh, my kid. . . ." and I'd say, "Oh, is that the thirteen-year-old?" And they got really interested in you if you were interested in what they said. So in the end they all came around.

The younger guys, I met on their same level as well, athletically. I decided to join their baseball team, and I made it. They even cut some guys on the side, but I still made the team, because I had the ability to make it, not because I blew the coach. (Laughter.) Contrary to popular thought.

So we all came together, kinda unified. In my first three months I think the basic thing in the whole mill was to take care of Joanne. Protect her. Cover her ass. Make sure she's okay.

Before, nobody was covering no one's ass, just their own. And nobody went out for beers with each other. Nobody. I got my three months' probation, I goes, "Hey, got my three months in, I'm going wild. Who's coming?" All of a sudden there's fifteen, twenty people at this bar. These people have never been drinking together before. They've been there ten, twenty years.

DEBBIE: Joanne is really loved by the people in her area. It's really nice. I've seen some of the guys with her. She's the biggest success story of any of the women of Stelco that I know. And it's because she's got a really outgoing personality, really wonderful, giving.

JOANNE: I've been competitive all my life, so I meet them on another level too. Now we have fights, constantly. "You can't lift that." "I'll bet you twenty bucks that I can lift that." All of a sudden there's eighteen people around. "All right, I've got ten on her, I've got five on her." You know what I mean? And I lift it up. And they freak. And I go down to the washroom. (Moans.) Like I died.

DEBBIE: It takes a big toll on you.

JOANNE: Yeah, it does. Because even though I'm getting on such a friendly basis with them, I'm still a woman. They treat me like one of the guys but they don't treat me like a guy. And that's the big difference. So I have to handle that. And then I come home and I gotta go to baseball. So I gotta put my uniform on and I know I can play well, but now I gotta play my absolute best just to look normal, like I fit in, right? And they're just playing their average. But I'm playing my best, so I don't embarrass them by playing rotten if it's an off day, right?

And then I gotta handle their wives. Their wives are constantly stabbing me in the back. Constantly. Not all of them. But there's some that really hate me, just because of what I represent, not because of who I am. So I gotta handle them.

I'm a big threat to them because I get along with the men so well. Like, they even say to me after work, "Come on, let's go for a beer." "Sure, no problem." But they never take their wives out for a beer. And we'll go to the parties. And I don't want to sit in the corner and talk about ring around the collar (laughter), so I'll shoot a game of pool with the men. Or have a beer. And again, they're threatened. You know what I mean? And if only they knew I envied their lives so much. Family, kids. But oh no, I'm the big hussy.

And then I gotta handle the men on the other team. And now it's getting so bad I gotta handle the wives of the men on the other team too. Men pick on your ability. If you cannot field the ball: "Hey, there's a hole at second base!" "You can't catch nothing!" But their wives! They yell: "Hey fatso." Or "Hey, streaks!" I got a beer gut. I got my hair streaked too. One woman, I wanted to punch her out. "Oh your stomach's getting a little big! What else do you like to do with the boys, streaks? Come on, can you hit the ball? Oh, you like balls, eh?" On and on. I'm like this (tenses her shoulders). I hit a triple and they shut up. Their husbands turn around and glare and they shut up.

DEBBIE: So what I'm saying is that you make it and you really survive, and if we were giving out badges, you'd get the Stelco badge, but you *pay* for it. Right? And people that don't worry so much about making everything good don't do so well.

Jeannette's also a big success story. From a different angle than Joanne's. She has some amazing stories about how she tells the younger guys, from the position of being a thirty-five-year-old mother, and yet also very attractive and young-looking —

JEANNETTE: Oh yes, of course. Some of the guys I work with went to school with my kids. We joke about it 'cause their friends ask me to go out on dates with them. One of the guys I work with jokingly calls me mom. He's always talking about cars with me, and he's a good friend of mine at work. But he was in my son's class at school. So it's interesting that way.

The guys come to me when they want something done, or when they want information on some of the gases, health and safety, or one of the guy's wife's miscarrying, he wants to see what I can do. They come to me when they want some help on a grievance. There aren't stewards around, so they'll come to me. I do get fed up. "For Christ-sakes. You guys have got to take the initiative. You're spending your life in here. I'm not going to be here forever. Why don't you do it?" And they say, "Hey, but we can't do it. We can't do it."

DEBBIE: My experience was different than Jeannette's. When we came in we knew more about the union than most people did. We'd been hanging around the union hall for months. Jeannette was able to use it in a good way, but I was aggressive about everything. I wanted things changed quickly. I went in like a ton of bricks: "We got to do all this the right way. We got to do this, we got to do that." It just didn't work.

There's no feeling for the union in my area, or very little. In fact, the guys are very hostile to the union because they think it has sold out the coke ovens over the years. I come in, wearing a union sticker on my hat. They would say, "Why are you wearing that union sticker? It's just a sellout union."

The health and safety conditions were disgusting, so I refused work a couple of times — the health and safety bill says that you can refuse unsafe work. The problem was that nobody else would refuse work with me. Whenever I'd make some kind of protest they'd say, "Oh, sure, you like doing this stuff. You like getting your name in the paper." So they saw me as somebody who was doing it for the publicity. I had a university

education so they figured I wasn't going to stay long. I was
mouthy as hell. I would fight. We would have knock-down,
drag-em-outs every day in the lunchroom about everything.
You know — Russia, cars. They all hated Ladas 'cause they
were communist cars. (Laughter.) And I would fight that. We'd
have fights about women, twenty guys and me, right? The
whole lunchroom. And at the time I thought it was kinda neat.
I thought I was doing a good job. And the guys sort of liked
that I fought. There were some very good moments.

But the overall impression by the end of it was that I was just
raising shit all the time for no reason. And in fact, when the
graffiti went on the wall about all the things I was — that I was
a lesbian and a commie and a cocksucker — they would add at
the bottom: "and a supporter of the union." (Laughter.) This
was as much an insult there as anything else.

The company set us up for this. They refused to give us our
own washroom. So the women in the coke ovens and the blast
furnaces used the same washroom as the men. If the men want
to have graffiti in their washroom that's their business, but not
with me using the same thing — there was all this graffiti from
before I was there. There were women's bodies sort of spread,
you know, and all kinds of what I consider anti-woman graffiti
— "Fuck the broad," and so on. Then they started using names.
There was this one student who was a bit chubby, and they put
up some graffiti about her. I would go in there and wipe it off.
Then one day it said, "A woman's place is in the home." And I
began to debate this. So we got into a graffiti war. I'd write: "A
woman's place is anywhere she wants to be." We'd go through
this, back and forth. And then it said: "A woman's place is at
home with her legs spread, unless she's prepared to come to
work and do the same." Well, that really escalated it for me. I
got really pissed off.

I used to tear down the beaver shots they put up in the
lunchroom, the nude beaver shots of women. And this would
outrage even the guys I was really close to, who were my
friends.

JEANNETTE: I have never torn one down. We went through this
whole thing with one of the women getting harassed because she
had taken a picture down. It got really bad — guys running a

pencil through a crotch shot in front of her face while she's trying to have coffee.

In one lunchroom, when I first started, there were wall-to-wall pictures. I was introduced to the guys there, went on the job, came back for a coffee break and every one of the pictures was gone. One of the older fellas had torn them down.

A lot of the guys will stick up for another guy who's got pictures on the wall, even though they themselves would never dream of putting one up. "That guy puts it up, it's his property." But I've seen guys take down a picture, fold it up and put it in a guy's locker. If a picture is really insulting.

JOANNE: This girl BJ did something really neat. In this one pulpit there was a really gross picture, eh? I saw it one day, and the next night I went in again and looked, and there was this little paper bikini taped to the girl's crotch. (Laughter.) And up on her top. And the guy sitting there goes, "They cleaned their act up." Later, BJ said she did it. The guys thought that was hilarious. Instead of ripping it down violently, she added to it. Turned it into something different.

DEBBIE: But we've talked about this again and again. To survive in there depends on extra special creativity, kindness. If I had worked at Stelco five years ago I would've been much more polite. But in recent years, as I've become more conscious of the way I repress anger as a woman, I'm trying to let it out more. When I started work at Stelco, I was just beginning to think about the fact that I never talked back to anybody. So I was gonna be angry. A guy made me angry, I said, "This makes me angry." Why shouldn't I do that?

It's a whole question of numbers. There's no group of women at Stelco who are really comfortable and are doing just what they want to do. They haven't hired enough women yet. Women are always having to think about how they're behaving.

There was one day on one shift when there were six students and two permanent women and we walked into the lunchroom and it was *our* lunchroom all of a sudden. There were ten guys and eight women. And we felt great. We were playing cards and making noise, and we really felt at home. After that we always noticed the difference. All the other times, there was just one or two of us. That's why I think a lot of women don't want to work there. There's lots of different ways of surviving, but there's no way of being completely comfortable. That's what brings on the tension, the pressure.

The whole question of whether we were women or not is a big issue. Guys keep on saying, "You're here. That means you're a guy." I'd say, "No, I'm a woman." They'd kid around with me about the pictures. "Hey, Field, you're here. You must like this type of thing. That's why you're here. You like this environment." And I'd say, "No, I don't like this environment. I'm not a man, I'm a woman. And if I had my way, I'd be treated like a woman. I think I'm equal. But for me, women's liberation doesn't mean I'm a man. It means I can do the same job as a man. And if I can do it, I can get the same wage. But I'm not the same."

We have a different culture, a woman's culture. I would like to be able to bring this women's culture into the plant. But we can't if it's just three or four women in every area. And that's why it makes me so angry that Stelco is not hiring more women, and why we got ourselves into this terrible bind.

We said Stelco should hire at least ten percent women. Now we're boxed in, because the number of new people being hired is such a small percentage of the thousands of workers here, and ten percent of that is miniscule. We'll never catch up.

Then we kept saying, "We want to be in all parts of the plant. No ghettoization."

JOANNE: I was in a mill all by myself for ten months and women were getting scattered — one here, another one over there. Instead of putting eight women in this mill, four in that mill, five in that one, they took three women and put them in a mill where there's never been women since the war, and put us all on different shifts. And we were the only women in there for ten months. It would be better to integrate a couple of mills.

JEANNETTE: Then the guys could see women as women work, as women talk together when they're working. Men don't see women working together, and how they talk when they work together. Because women traditionally work in job ghettos.

DEBBIE: I felt like I had no sexuality. Like I was not allowed. It was partly because of what I wore — seven layers. I felt like a blob, a fat little round blob with a hood and a helmet. I felt like I couldn't touch anybody, couldn't put my arm around anybody, couldn't flirt with anybody. I felt like it was all off limits. I had to just be a eunuch. That was the only way I could survive.

JEANNETTE: For me it took a while. You know, you hug and kiss in my family, especially at Christmas. You don't think twice about it. But at work everybody says, "Merry Christmas, Jeannette," and they shake your hand. I'm going like this (opens up arms for a kiss). Three hundred Merry Christmases and you're holding yourself back.

But now the guys ask me to go out with them. A few of them have said to me, "All along I wanted to take you out, but I didn't know how you felt about going out with somebody." I said, "Well, I haven't gone out with anybody in the department because of talk." But now, yes, a guy will give me a kiss, a guy will put his arm around me, rub my hair — "How 'ya doing Jeannette?" This type of thing. We're comfortable with each other now. We're not afraid to touch each other. They're not afraid you're gonna cry, "Harassment!"

One thing I still have a problem with, though. I don't wear a bra at work, because it ruins your bras. In the lunchroom, here I sit with my T-shirt on and over it my jacket, because if I take it off, my nipples will show. This is a real problem. The guys take their T-shirts off and sit there bare-chested, because the blast furnaces are really hot. So what do you do?

But this fear of touching, that's gone now. It's all more normal. It's worked itself out.

JOANNE: With me it was like that right off the bat. But just with the older guys. They were always hugging me. I'd come out of the sewer soaking wet, like a rat. They'd make me tea and that. It's always been that way. I look at the guys now, hug them, tickle them if they're in the middle of doing a job, right?

JEANNETTE: Yeah, but the women need to discuss these things. Discussing it makes you more relaxed and comfortable with it, because every woman's gone through the same thing. Even a guy's gone through the same thing. One guy said, "Christ, I've got to buy new work clothes 'cause I can't have a ripped crotch with the women around." So it is an issue that should be handled. The women's committee should handle that. That's one of a million things that we need to talk about on the women's committee.

DEBBIE: A few months after we were hired we were having trouble with the washrooms and with women trying to get transfers to other departments. We went to the union. We had a women's committee before, we knew how good it was, so we wanted to form one within the union. What we really should have done, and still should do, is gotten the women together informally at somebody's house to talk about some kind of structure of women. Instead we went through the local, and we got a committee formed in a very stilted way inside the union bureaucracy. We had four women appointed and three men . . .

JEANNETTE: Three watchdogs. . . .

DEBBIE: . . . on our committee. And everything we did needed approval. We couldn't go anywhere. It just didn't take off. And the big problem was to get the women out to it. Joanne's a perfect example. She came with a lot of energy, really gung ho, but she was disappointed.

JOANNE: I was going for a fight, man. I was tooth and nail behind everybody, anybody that had anything to gain by it, men as well. And I get to this meeting and I know maybe two people there. Debbie's up there and Jeannette, and I see this man on the other side of the room. I don't know him from a hole in the wall. Why are men here? And I thought, That's a nice idea, men coming here. And these women are getting up and discussing what happened to them when they first started, and why they're being harassed, and why the company is trying to split the men and the women, right?

And the man across the room, he's got this suit on and he's sitting like this (crosses her legs, leans back). And he's got a nail clipper. All you hear is: *Snap. Snap. Snap.* And when all these women were speaking, he had no inclination to listen. Then he stood up and went on and on. He said nothing for an hour. He wasted an hour of crucial time of the first meeting these women ever had.

DEBBIE: This committee met quite regularly for four or five months. And then everything got stopped because of contract negotiations. We had two general meetings after that, and about twenty women came. What we were really banking everything on was transforming the committee into a bigger thing where people could talk and really get some solutions to their problems.

JEANNETTE: We need a women's committee to solve our problems, to do a little bit of work within the local, to make the women's situation better and, if nothing else, to have a beer together and talk over our experiences. We need this interaction. I need it as a woman, interaction with other women, regardless of the union or anything. We're not going to get that, though, through formal meetings at the hall with our watchdogs and a chairperson. We're going to do it through subtler ways, like a woman's party, a shower for one of the women in the plant who's getting married.

One funny thing. I had a call from one of our watchdogs on the executive a couple of weeks ago. He suggested that the women's committee should organize daycare for strikers on strike duty. I said, "You mean the women of the plant should set up something for the men and women's children? There isn't a woman in the plant that I know of that needs daycare. But a lot of guys in my department do. Let me think about it." 'Cause I was just fuming. I thought about it. But I didn't want the name of the women's committee connected in any way to any daycare and sandwich making. In this situation we were strikers first. In another situation, fine. I don't mind looking after kids, but in this situation I am a striker. Our place is on the picket line as picketers. And we should be recognized as such.

JOANNE: You're okay as long as you keep your place. They just keep ramming that down your throat.

JEANNETTE: We've been ignored by the press and in all the publicity about that strike. It's as if there isn't a woman striker in existence. Women are on picket duty. If there's a woman there, everybody just assumes it's a wife. The natural thing would be to assume that she's a woman steelworker if she's walking on the picket line with a sign, but we've been completely ignored.

JOANNE: What they're going to end up with is the same package that we had when we went in. And they're talking about contract language, changing it from "he" to "person" or "he and she."

Who cares? We know "he" applies to us. Why don't they just change it all to "person," over and done with, bang, next issue. But no. How many weeks did they spend on that?

JEANNETTE: It's a joke. All the real women's issues got shelved.

I think working at Stelco has made me a real feminist. It's thrown in my face that I have to be one, just to survive. I don't want to end up falling into the trap of staying at Stelco all my life. Even if I'm there two years, it's a high price to pay for this issue that didn't really get solved. I feel I have to finish up the women's committee before I leave, make sure it gets off the ground the way the women want it, not the way the executive does.

JOANNE: Basically, what it's really done is show me how to fight and where my priorities lie. Most of it has nothing to do with Stelco, but if it wasn't for Stelco I probably wouldn't have ever found those out, those facts about myself.

It's affected my dad too. It was always his sons, his sons, his sons. And I've shown him that you don't have to be a man in order to work in a man's environment or compete in a man's field. Even though we argue a lot more about work, he's starting to see.

He knows there's discrimination, he knows how we get treated, but this foreman's bullshit's always been in his brain. Now there's cobwebs around it. That's how settled it is. And now I'm coming up to him and I'm the exact same way he was when he was a kid. He's seeing himself in me, which totally freaks him out.

DEBBIE: I think what being at Stelco has taught me was some of the problems with the kind of heavy-handed top-down notion of political leadership that I had. Which is the notion that you have a leader — the union leader, the left-wing leader, a feminist leader — and that person has a truth, and they give the recipe for the truth, and other people get the truth, and they throw up a big struggle and the world changes. That doesn't work.

Real political leadership has a lot to do with the heart as well as the mind. It has a lot to do with loving people that you're struggling with. "You're my brother, you're my buddy. We're on the team together. Stop being such an asshole." You know? While with me it was more like I was somebody from outside telling them what to do, and the reaction I got was, "Leave me alone. Fuck off. You can't tell me this stuff."

I learned that I want to act and listen to my heart a lot more, because a lot of really good things happened at Stelco amongst people. A lot of warm, moving experiences happened when I didn't exclude myself. I played cards, I learned to play cards really well at Stelco, and every once in a while it would snap and I would be one of the guys, just playing cards, you know?

It's raised a lot of questions for me about the future. For all three of us. What kind of jobs do we want? We know the problems of being a woman in our present situation. On the other hand, Joanne would hate a dress and nylons and having to "yes-sir-no-sir" to a boss in an office. You'd go out of your mind. Could I work in a typing pool? Could any of us work in a typing pool? What are the alternatives?

JOANNE: That's the struggle: Woman, can you make it? At the end of the struggle, do you have that choice? Can you leave, or do you have to stay?

JEANNETTE: The guys give up and stay forever. And give it their whole body. Their body rots.

DEBBIE: Which is one of the reasons the guys are hostile towards us. It's dirty. It's got terrible shifts and terrible time off. So you do this and what do you get in return? You get not a great wage, but a relatively better wage. You do that basically because you're supporting a family. I mean, there's maybe one out of a hundred, a guy who stayed there for twenty years who wasn't married and had a family. Then you see a woman coming in. And you realize that she can work. And that breaks up that whole thing. It throws a rock into that whole circle that you've got going. Every morning you say to yourself, "I can't stand this job, but I gotta go in, 'cause I gotta support the wife and kids." Well, if the wife can work, then it destroys the whole argument. So we are a tremendous threat to that.

JEANNETTE: Also, I think they are threatened that this woman could leave in a year or two and raise her own family. She got out. She's free.

DEBBIE: That whole pattern — you're born, you go to work at Stelco, you stay there for thirty-five years — women being there challenged all that.

I had a fight with this one guy. He used to always say, "I can't stand it here. I can't stand coming in." And I would say to him, "Well, does your wife work?" And he'd say, "No fucking way I'd ever let my wife work. No way." I'd say to him, "Look. If your wife would work, you could take some time off. And you could look for a better job. A different job. My working here gives you freedom." He used to get so pissed off.

That's probably why the wives are very threatened as well.

DEBBIE: Yes, because it means that they might have to go to work too.

JOANNE: I think so. I never thought of that. It makes sense.

DEBBIE: It shakes up everything.

Jeannette and Joanne were laid off shortly after the strike ended. Jeannette is currently unemployed, though hoping to go back to work at Stelco. Joanne is vice-president of Hamilton's union of the unemployed. Debbie is working at the Development Education Centre in Toronto.

Squidjiggers Loretta Burt and Betty Burt
in Carter's Cove, New World Island,
Newfoundland

SQUIDJIGGING WOMEN

BETTY BURT
&
LORETTA BURT

BETTY WAS DOING hairdressing out of her home in Carter's Cove in the summer of 1977 when the squid started rolling ashore. Like hundreds of other women on the north coast of Newfoundland, she decided the squid were a good way to make some more money. When Loretta returned from St. John's at the end of that summer, Betty convinced her that they should invest in a boat for the following year. The price paid for the squid wasn't much, but it was better than occasional hairdressing and, like men fishing in Canada, they looked forward to unemployment insurance to take them through the winter months.

Betty is married to Loretta's brother. They live across the road from one another and are good friends.

BETTY: My grandfather was a fisherman and my father was a fisherman. He did lobster fish and cod fish; he didn't do much squid. But anything else. It must be twenty years ago I used to go out to the traps with him, lobster fishing. Didn't go out again until 1977.

The reason why we started was so many squids come ashore on the beach. They were rolling on the beach. And they were rotting there, just lying there and rotting. So we decided to take them up and clean them. We didn't go into it big that year, just a few squid.

LORETTA: I was living in St. John's that summer. When I came home I could smell it, eh? (Laughs.) We drove through the community and I had to come in and ask what it was, the smell, because that's the first time the squids have hit the shore for *years.* I lived here all my life and that's the first time I remember it being like that, eh?

BETTY: We didn't go in the boat at all the first year, we just picked them up off the beach. And when we saw how much money we could make at it, and they were only eighty cents a pound that year, well the next year we got ready to go squid-jigging. I talked Lora into it, and told her that she *had* to go, because there was nobody else to go with me. So we got a boat and got a motor and away we went.

LORETTA: I said I wouldn't go and be at it, because it seemed like just too yucky! (Laughs.) But I tried it the next year.

The first day, Betty left twelve squid on a piece of board down in the basement for me to clean next morning. I wouldn't let her come down and see me pipping the squid because I know she'd make fun at me, eh? So I just went down and started doing it myself to see if I could do it, eh? And time I got through the ten, 'leven squids, I was very good.

It was hard, but it was something to do, something to make money, eh? The only way that you can make money around here, unless you've got education, work in a store or something like that.

BETTY: You're out there when it gets daylight. And it don't make that much difference about the tides. Sometimes the squid'll jig at low tide, other times it's high tide, so it really don't matter. Well, if you've got to go out in the rainy weather, you go out in it; we don't go out when it's blowing hard, unless we take some men. (Laughs.)

You jig with a squid reel, and it's just a big bulky drum that weighs about, oh, about a hundred pound, probably. And there's lines attached with about eighty jiggers on it, wound up on the drum. And you just unwind them down over the side of the boat. There's about twenty or twenty-five hooks on each jigger. You lower that over the side of the boat and you start jigging and you wait for the squid to come. You just reel it back and forth, back and forth so that the lines are jiggling up and down, and the red squid jigger, that's what toles the squid. He sees the colour of that and comes after it. It'll go after it with his mouth, but it's not very often you jig it by the mouth; you usually jig it by the side.

Sometimes you can go out and be out there ten minutes and load the boat, but other times you could go out ten days and not get a squid.

LORETTA: Which has been happening this year, eh? It's been happening a lot this year we can't get them.

BETTY: If you go out at five in the morning, you'll get in about eight-thirty, nine o'clock. If you go out at five in the evening, you get in around ten or ten-thirty at night.

LORETTA: And that's about the times you usually do go out, eh? It's not very often you'll go out in the day. Not in the middle of the day. They don't seem to be jigging all that. This is the time they usually jig, eh? Early in the morning or in the evening.

Oh, it's really something. You get out there in the boat in the mornings, you watch the sun come up and it's really beautiful. I've had to use the flashlight this year, when we've went out, eh? To get down the boat and everything.

This year I went out by myself. Well, I didn't really leave the wharf alone.

One morning I got up and I went out with two people. One fellow got in the boat with me, and the other one got in his own boat. But when we got down to the squid jigging ground at the time, they left and went on in search of more squid somewhere else. I stayed there, like, and anchored off and jigged. I was out there by meself, anchored off, and there's around five or six men over there, in sight. And by and by the squids took hold to mine, and I started pulling them aboard. Up comes this man behind me. "Hey, skipper!" he said, "can I tie onto you?" And I turned around, and he said, "My Gahd!" he said, "it's a *woman!*" (Laughs.)

Well, he tied on. But he didn't get anything afterwards. He just cut off. That was all the squids I got for that day too. The next evening I went out, back at another place where you usually catch squid, and I heard him telling the men about this, eh? "When I went up to tie on . . ."

I don't usually go out by myself. I mean, I've used the engine and went out, me and another woman, eh? Me and Bet, me and Marian up on the hill, we just steamed out there, eh? But I haven't went no great distance, because I'm not used to it, eh? Well, you see, you didn't have to go out as far as the men. You can see the squid jiggin' ground, eh, right out there. (Points.)

You're all tied boat for boat. There's a lot of boats sometimes, maybe fifty boats. There's one over here, maybe, and one there, and a couple there —

BETTY: When we come in, we tie up the boat to the side of the wharf. And then we got to get buckets, because the government hasn't seen fit to give us a hoist to put on the wharf (laughs), so we got to use five-gallon buckets with a piece of rope on. One of us stays in the boat and puts the squid in the bucket; the other one stays on the wharf and pulls the bucket full of squid up over the wharf, until we get them all up. That takes about an hour, hour and a half. And then we start to pip 'em.

You got to slit the head and slit the gut (sighs), take out the pip — that's what the gut is called — take out the two eyes and the biter; and then we have to wash it in about three waters, because there's a lot of black ink that comes out of a squid. And after we get it washed, then there's another hour to clean up the wharf, clean off the table, load it aboard the truck, bring it in the garden, unload it and hang it on the line —

LORETTA: And this is where your work *begins.* (Laughs.)

BETTY: Now the work begins, when you gets it on the line. First you prays there's no rain, and then you starts your work.

You have to do a lot of praying in Newfoundland! (Laughter.)

BETTY: That's the most we do, is pray. Lora here takes care of that! (Laughs.)

LORETTA: I haven't been very successful this year, have I!

Well, you hang them up, right? You take them from the truck and hang them up in the garden. You have your lines all out, right? Or you can have flakes — that's chicken wire strung up off the ground — and you put them on there. And you just hang them on the line as if they're going to sleep, their backs down on the line.

Then you leave them alone. They'll dry up, if it's a nice day, in two or three hours.

BETTY: Usually we hangs them out in the night, so the next morning —

LORETTA: It's dried up. But if it's in the morning, well, it hangs about two or three hours. Just enough so you can hang up the two longest tentacles. We usually takes them and throws them over the line, don't we? So then they won't stick together. If the heads stick together, they get pink quicker, they spoil. So every one of the horns, we call them — tentacles — every one we pick apart, and hang them by the head. Everybody's got a different way of doing it, eh? Whatever they finds easier, they do. But this is the way we usually do it. And then we left them alone. If we suspects rain we take them in. Then they got to be taken in, put out, taken in, put out!

That's a lot of work for your eighty cents a pound.

BETTY: The second year we got $2.30. I made about $3,500, in August, September, October — three months.

LORETTA: I made about the same, because we went together. We went partners. But last year we only got a dollar-ten. And I worked like a dog! And this year now we're getting two dollars again, but we're getting no squid.

And then — well, didn't you pack them? Whoever you're

selling to, they give you boxes. Well, that year we had to take them to the plant ourselves and wait sometimes an hour or longer, and then sometimes they wouldn't be there. They'd be going out to dinner or something like that, eh? You'd have to come back. But, now, this year they've sent around collectors. They'll come to your door and take your squid, give you your money and that's it. They've got their own trucks and everything, so you can see the money that's in it.

The men used to sell the squid to these foreign ships which used to come in. The men used to take them out, and if they couldn't get rid of them, they used to dry them, I guess, and their wife help them. Not in my case, because my husband wasn't fishing then, eh? But the women, they didn't used to sell them to the boats, eh? That was too easy! (Laughs.) The women weren't going to get off so easy as that! (Laughs.) We had to bring them ashore and start from there. In bad weather that's sometimes a week, week and a half job, isn't it?

BETTY: Yes.

LORETTA: Sometimes you got to bring them in the storehouse, light a fire on them to dry them.

BETTY: But there's something else too. It don't run as easy as that. The first day when we get our squid, we do what we just told you we do. Well, they're on the line. The second morning we go out and get more squid. And when we come in, if we've got any squid partly drying in the storehouse, we don't clean the fresh catch until we hangs those out. Well, then when we've got the partly dry ones out, we got to clean the ones we got on the wharf! (Laughs.) Yes, we do. So we clean them and we wash them and bring them in. Well, time we get in, and ones we hung up the day before — not the ones we took out of store, but our green ones from the day before — it's time to turn them over. After that we got to hang out the ones we just brought in! And by the time we get those hung out, it's time to take our driest ones into the storehouse. And that's how it goes from day to day.

LORETTA: From week to week. I've had to take them and dump them when they've gone bad. I've had to take them off the line, after working two or three days at them, and carry them out to the well barn and dump them in the water. I've had to do that. When the weather have been bad and you haven't been able to save them, and you've had to take them out and dump them.

BETTY: After you get three days rain on it.

LORETTA: It's not much hope.

BETTY: You could dry it, probably, and cover it up, but it wouldn't be fit to eat. This year have been the worst one, weather-wise and squid-wise too.

You gets up at five in the morning, and you probably get to bed twelve in the night, because every spare minute you got, you've got to be in the shed packing some for to sell.

Thirty-five hundred dollars doesn't seem like a lot of money for that amount of work.

BETTY: It don't seem like a lot of money, but it was a lot of money to us at the time. We weren't making any money at all, and all of a sudden to get that money, it was luck.

Everybody wanted the money, and at that time we were told that we could collect unemployment insurance. That give us a boost.

LORETTA: More eager to get at it, eh?

BETTY: We worked about fifteen weeks altogether. In a fisherman's case, he can work when he like. Well, he works the full summer. And when he sells, it don't make any difference when he gets paid for it, as far as unemployment insurance is concerned. If he says this is my work for three weeks, he get three unemployment stamps, because that was his work for three weeks and nobody questions it. And probably he would go back again in three more weeks time and sell again and say this is for three weeks. And everything would be fine. So we did the same thing. We probably sold $700 worth of squid at one time, after three or four weeks work, and we were expecting three or four unemployment stamps. So we filed our claim like everybody else.

At that time you had to have ten stamps to make a claim. It averaged out that we had fourteen or fifteen weeks altogether, and the squid buyers thought the same as we did, that we had the same rights as the men. So we filed our claim when the men filed theirs, and the men got their report cards back, and the women got a letter: "Your claim is under study. A decision will be made shortly."

Well, the men got their unemployment, and the women that had a man's name, such as Georgie, Frances, they got their unemployment. But every other woman got a letter saying they were under study. And about two weeks later we got a letter saying that it was turned over to Revenue Canada and they were going to investigate. So that was okay, we didn't say anything about the investigation. But after a month or so, nothing was coming out of it, so we started to phone the unemployment office. Well, no good phoning there. "We got nothing to do with it, it got turned over to Revenue Canada."

Well, we didn't think much about it because we were that used to women not getting anything. Because we just thought that's the way it had to be. The men were entitled to it but the women weren't, eh?

They turned it over to Revenue Canada, and then they started to phone, asking questions. "Did you jig your own squids? Have you got a boat? Have you got a fishing licence? Who was in the boat with you when you jigged the squids? Did anybody help you? What body of water did you jig the squids in? How large was the body of water?"

They were really trying to stall us. So then we called our MP, Mr. George Baker. He's a Liberal. (Laughs.) So he played around with it for a long, long time. Finally he called back. He had everything straightened out. "You're going to get your unemployment." Good. "Because we're not calling it a dry fish now, we're calling it a wet one." (Laughs.)

LORETTA: Our dry squid now all of a sudden got wet.

What did they mean?

BETTY: I don't know what they meant. (Laughs.) But if that was the only way we could get it . . .

LORETTA: . . . we're willing to go along with them.

BETTY: We said okay! We don't care if it's called wet or dry, we'll take the money.

Another two or three weeks went by and we didn't hear

anything from our unemployment, so we started phoning again, and not getting no information. So at that time, four of us decided we'd take a trip to St. John's to find out what was going on.

We went to St. John's, and we went to the Revenue Canada office. They had a man in there from Ottawa to determine whether we were entitled to it or not.

First we weren't allowed in the office — no way, not going to even look at you, eh? We had got up at three o'clock in the morning and drove to Gander and took a flight to St. John's with our own money, and had to come back again that evening, and now they're not going to tell us anything.

LORETTA: They threatened the cops on us if we didn't leave. So we got our dander up then.

BETTY: We said, "We're *not* (thumps the table) leaving until our files are took out on this table, and we'll look at them together. And then you can give us an answer, whether we're entitled to it or not. And whatever that answer is, we're satisfied to go." So, I mean, the fellow from Ottawa almost messed his pants! (Laughs.) He turned all red and kind of got scared. He didn't know what we were going to do with him.

They had boxes of files there about two feet high, tied up in rope and put back in the corner. They untied the boxes. And then they told us one of us was going to get our unemployment! That woman from Twillingate, she qualified. She was going to get it.

LORETTA: That was after they felt her arm.

BETTY: He didn't think that she had muscles enough in her arm to be a real fisherman, you know.

LORETTA: She's a small woman, eh? But she can work!

BETTY: He felt to see if she had any muscles in her arm. He said, "I don't know . . ." Now, he should have felt mine!

LORETTA: So then he says the rest of us were not entitled to it, we didn't have weeks enough. They saw where we made the big shipments, and they just give us one stamp for each.

BETTY: Yes, it didn't matter how many weeks' work was in each shipment, we just got the one stamp, that's all. So that satisfied us at the time. They didn't kick us out that time, did they?

So when we left his office, we didn't have anything else to do, since we couldn't get our flight out before late in the night. So we went to our MHA, Bill Rowe, to kill time. When we got there and was talking about it, he didn't agree with Revenue Canada's decision. He thought that they should space out the stamps the same as they did for the fishermen. So we talked it over and that, and then he called up a radio hotline show, and arranged for us to tell our story. So we went there.

LORETTA: We were supposed to come into this office, now, all riled up and mad — which we were, eh? But by the time we got there, we was kind of nervous about doing this thing, getting on the air. The other two ladies wouldn't go on. So Bet went on first and then I went on.

BETTY: We were on most of an hour.

What kind of response did you get from people phoning in?

BETTY: (Laughs.) We didn't get much, because a man burst in and demanded that we get our unemployment. He came to this station where we were on the hotline, eh?

LORETTA: He came and he got on the radio too. (Laughs.)

BETTY: He took over!

BETTY: When we came down from the interview there was somebody waiting for us from the CBC. We went to the CBC, and like a lot of people, they didn't believe that we were doing the work. They definitely didn't believe that we were going out in the boat. They thought we were all fishermen's wives, and our husbands was going out in the boat and doing all the work and shipping the fish and giving us stamps to let us collect unemployment insurance.

LORETTA: Both our husbands are carpenters.

BETTY: And one of the men working at the CBC felt my coat, and because it was a leather coat, he more or less thought that I didn't deserve unemployment insurance.

LORETTA: Tell her how you got your coat, Betty! (Laughs.)

BETTY: I got it on sale because it had a rip in it, and I sewed up the rip. So it didn't cost me that much. .

And then we got a call from Mayor Dorothy Wyatt. She

phoned and invited us out. She wanted to know all about what this was going on.

This day must have been a pretty heady day for you, was it?

BETTY: It was good. We en*joy*ed it.

LORETTA: We got it off our chests, eh, some of the things that was building up over the period when we was home waiting. More or less shot off it some! (Laughs.) It felt good, you know?

BETTY: That started it up again. People told us they didn't think it was right. If the men could collect unemployment insurance that way, why couldn't women? And it was not only women telling us, it was men too.

That started us rolling again then. Like, all the women were interested in it, but they didn't have the guts to talk about it on the radio or TV or anywhere. They'd phone me and Lora all the time, but as for doing anything theirself, they wouldn't do it. Before we went to St. John's, we had phoned every woman we could think of to go along with us, because the more we had, we felt, the better it would be. But we ended up with four of us, that's all we got to go.

So when we came back home, we called a meeting in Virgin Arm. The first one. We got organized that night and we went from there.

LORETTA: We formed a group, the Notre Dame Squid Women, we called it. Betty was the president, I was the secretary and Joyce Harvey was the treasurer.

BETTY: When we left St. John's I told the Revenue guy from Ottawa that I would see him in Ottawa, and he didn't believe it. So as soon as we got organized, we started raising the funds to go to Ottawa. And at the same time, the Status of Women was after hearing about us. Lynn Verge (In Status of Women as well as Minister of Education, Newfoundland Legislature) contacted Lora and offered her a free trip to Ottawa to tell her story about discrimination.

LORETTA: They booked appointments for us, eh?

BETTY: So we got busy to raise money to send two more people up, because we thought the more the better, right?

We went to all the businesses, we went to all our family, all our friends, and asked for a dollar, two dollars, whatever they mind to give. And the businesses were good, and most of them gave ten dollars, twenty dollars, except one cheapskate, he give a dollar! That's the fellow who we buys our liquor from! (Laughs.)

LORETTA: I don't buy liquor, so —

BETTY: And we raised over a thousand dollars. It took about three weeks. Everybody was interested in it at this time, eh? And the majority of people wanted us to go. Neither of us wanted to go. I mean, we wanted to go for the trip, but we didn't want to go to do the talking and the arguing. But nobody else would do it, so we went. Me and Lora and Mary Burt. Three Burts! (Mary isn't related.)

LORETTA: Mary's a real good speaker, eh?

BETTY: She's not afraid to get up in a public place, where there were a lot of people, and talk. That's something I couldn't do. Well, Mary took that part of it. We used to go over everything before she got up, to get in everything in the few minutes you got, tell all the good points.

Well, we called George Baker — he was in Ottawa at the time — and told him we were coming. He didn't believe us. I asked him would he be in Ottawa or Gander, because I told him I had the feeling if he knew we were coming he'd be in Gander. (Laughs.) And we wanted him in Ottawa. So I give him the name of the hotel, and I told him what time we'd be there, and that we wanted him to be there when we got there, because we wanted to talk to him. He was our member of parliament so we needed him. He showed up. He didn't do anything for us, but he showed up. (Laughs.)

LORETTA: It was brought up in the House. [Parliament]

BETTY: By a Conservative member from St. John's. And we met Ed Broadbent. He was the most interested in our case of all we met. We met all the NDP crowd, all of them were interested. And we met Don Jamieson. He was from Newfoundland, the External Affairs minister. He promised us everything and gave us nothing.

LORETTA: Cup of tea.

BETTY: Yes, he did give us a cup of tea, and took our picture. Shaking hands. (Laughs.) The ones that were least interested were the Liberals, because they were in power at the time, so they didn't want to hear anything about it.

LORETTA: We met with taxation members, in Ottawa.

BETTY: We met with Mr. Bud Cullen, he was the Minister of — must have been Employment. He was one smart-alec. He didn't believe one word we had to say. Just the way he talked, this smirky look on his face, as if, "For God's sakes, stop telling your lies." We had an appointment to be in a meeting with him, and when we got there, there was about thirty more people there, and he give us about one minute to ask a question, and he give us one question. And I don't remember if I ever did get an answer, he just changed the subject.

LORETTA: The TV were there when we came out of the taxation office. They were there when we came out of the Human Rights place, they were in the Human Rights place with us, following us around.

BETTY: We got to talk to everyone we wanted to see, except the Minister of Fisheries. Everything was perfect, until the Liberals decided to call an election the same day.

LORETTA: We said they'd just done it so they wouldn't have to hear no more! We were getting all this publicity, eh? And then all of a sudden — election.

BETTY: You haven't heard the best one yet. We had a meeting with the Minister of Revenue Canada, and he was really good. He understood our problem. We told him that the people they had working in St. John's did not understand our problem, and they didn't. The most they knew how to do was sit on their ass and answer the telephone. They didn't know what a squid was, they didn't know the manner of work involved or anything. So he understood all that, we explained it to him, and he decided to send people down and really check into it and see what was going on. And he promised us by the end of May — this was after going through November, December, January, February and March — we'd have our answers.

This was the end of March. And he said he thought that if what we were telling was true, all the squid women would qualify for unemployment insurance. And we came home, and I was talking to Revenue Canada later, and I asked them about it. And they said that 99.9 percent of all women would qualify for unemployment insurance.

But in a matter of three days everything changed again. There was more than fifty percent qualified. I'd say there was about sixty percent. And then about twenty percent more took it to the Appeal Board before the Supreme Court, and they won. Lora and I didn't.

We didn't appeal it. Because by this time, we was more of a hindrance to the women than we was a help. We had the feeling, if we appealed it, nobody would win. But if they done it theirselves, and there was no Betty Burt or Loretta Burt there, that they probably would win it.

LORETTA: I knew the women worked and they deserved it, eh? No more than I deserved it or Betty deserved it, eh? But I really think they were entitled to it. I was really proud that they got it, eh? Although I was hurt that I didn't get mine, because I worked too.

BETTY: We talked it over, just the two of us. If we'd wanted, we wouldn't have lost anything. All the women were satisfied to give us part of their unemployment.

LORETTA: They really were.

BETTY: When we got the answer back from Revenue Canada, that sixty percent had qualified, we called another meeting, and we got Bill Rowe and George Baker out there again. Our biggest issue then was, if we didn't qualify now, next year is going to be worse. We had heard a rumour that it was going to be changed to twenty stamps. And they told us that that was bull. We would not need twenty stamps. So I said if they were talking about it, there was going to be something come out of it. "Naw, forget it; you won't need twenty stamps." Well, we damn well did need twenty stamps the following year.

LORETTA: I didn't even bother to try.

BETTY: In the meantime, a provincial election came up. And the fellow who works in the unemployment office ran for the PCs in our district. Now there's a lot of PCs in Carter's Cove, and he didn't come to visit his people, because somebody said that I had threatened to throw a bucket of water over him. (Laughs.) Well, you see, I never — not that I wouldn't do it — but I never said I'd do it. So some of the people were putting the blame on me and Lora because he didn't come to visit his people. So I phoned him up and asked him did he intend to come to Carter's Cove, and he said yes. And I told him what I heard, and that he was free to come, I wouldn't touch him. (Laughs.) So in fifteen minutes flat he was over. And he stopped out here, and he was going to come in the garden, but I wouldn't let him in. I told him I would talk to him on the road. So me and Lora went out to the drive, and of course first thing we asked him about was unemployment insurance.

He said that if he was elected, we would have no problems with unemployment insurance. Uh-huh. Now he was the man at the unemployment insurance office that said we didn't deserve it in the beginning. He belongs on this island, and he was the one that said, "No, they don't deserve it, they shouldn't get it." So he said that if we called a meeting and got all the Squid Women — because there were about two hundred of us at this time — to give their support to him, he said, "I guarantee you your unemployment." Lora said, "How come we didn't get it last year?" And he said, "George Baker could have got it for you with a five-minute phone call, that's all it would take."

And I said, "What about if we don't call a meeting and support you?" He said, "You'll never draw unemployment insurance."

I told him that we had one blank in St. John's like him and we didn't need another one. No way would I call a meeting. And he said, "Well, you'll never draw unemployment insurance." And I said, "Yes I will," because I was sure I would, because I had checked into it. And Lynn Verge had helped us, and she was in the provincial government. And he said, "Your friend Lynn Verge might be in St. John's sitting in the provincial government, but Ian Small's in the unemployment office, and you will *not* draw unemployment insurance." Well, I laughed at him, because I knew I was going to get unemployment insurance (laughs), because I had everything it took to qualify. Until I applied.

I went in to the office to sign up for unemployment insurance. I asked the clerk if I was eligible for it, and she told me
yes. I left and came home, and I waited for the report cards.
And I got them, with a notice saying, "Your claim is under
study. A decision will be made shortly." When the time was up,
I filled in the report cards and sent them back. And I got
another one back. "Your claim is under study." And I filled
that one out and sent it back. I got another notice. So I filled
that one out and sent it back, and I got a cheque. Saturday
morning. So I went to Lewisporte, shopping. (Laughs.) Monday morning I had another cheque. And Thursday I got
another cheque, and my report cards to send back. I sent them
back and I was supposed to get a cheque on the following
Thursday. I didn't get one. I waited until Monday and I didn't
get it. So I phoned the unemployment office and asked them
what happened. "You didn't get a cheque," she said, "because
you're not entitled to it." And I said, "Well, I'm after getting
two and a half," and she said, "No you didn't," and I said, "Yes,
I did," and she said, "No you didn't," and I said, "Okay, I
didn't!"(Laughs.) And she said, "Well, if you did, you got to
pay it back." And I said, "You just told me I didn't get it."

I had eleven stamps, had worked that year and had drawn
unemployment the year before, and I didn't qualify. But
women that had never worked before in their lives and had ten
stamps signed on and qualified, when actually they should have
needed twenty, because they never ever worked before. But
theirs was okay. And the ones that qualified was the same people
that worked for the fellow from unemployment in his election.
They worked and carried round his papers and they qualified.

Now they're threatening to take me to court. They've contacted the bank to pass over my money. I've got nine dollars there.
I don't know if the bank'll give them that or not. Not too worried. They keeps threatening to send me to court. But they
won't do it. I wish they would. I'd like to have it out in the
court.

LORETTA: I didn't apply for unemployment that year, because
I didn't think 'twas possible. I didn't have twenty stamps. But I
seen women did get their unemployment. What they did was

they didn't ship their squids all at one time. So next year I said, well, I'm going to try.

I held back the squid. Each week I only shipped enough for one stamp, eh? And then I ship another week, and I ship the same thing for another stamp — like that, eh? And they couldn't understand how I could ship the same amount like that each week. The squids was always the same price last year, $1.10. It never went up, eh? Which was tough, because the year before I would have got twice the amount of money, and I wouldn't have had to get so many squid, eh? But that year I had to get more squid, for less money.

I worked right up till the last couple of weeks in November. Certainly everybody in the Cove knows what I did, eh? Opened up the tentacles in the snow with the snow drifting in my face and the whole thing. I'd never do it again. Well, I signed up, and I got me unemployment, eh? Well, now I think they're doing an investigation, because they haven't bothered me at all, other than two or three months ago, there was —

BETTY: A plainclothesman, a cop.

LORETTA: Yes, I got his number. He was doing an investigation on this.

Would you say unemployment insurance helps you get a fair wage for your labour?

BETTY: Well, if it wasn't for unemployment, there wouldn't be able to be any fishermen. There's no way they could live. In the last month and a half now the fishermen haven't made a hundred and fifty dollars, and that's the biggest majority of them.

LORETTA: And they go down to try to get social assistance from the welfare, and they turn them away. They won't have nothing to do with them. Men from Summerford and surrounding areas went down and they won't *look* at them. They won't have *nothing* to do with them at all.

BETTY: So if they didn't have their unemployment insurance to look forward to in November, there's no way they could stay fishing. They would have to leave and do something else.

BETTY: I learned *never* to trust nobody in government. (Laughs.) 'Specially not in the unemployment office. I'd starve before I'd apply for unemployment insurance again. And I wouldn't let them get the six hundred dollars back.

If I phone the unemployment office and I don't give my name, they're as friendly as can be. But let me phone and give my name and they turned loose, as far as I'm concerned.

LORETTA: I wish I could change me name! (Laughs.)

BETTY: "You're one of those Burts, eh?"

It's like this: if you want something bad enough, you got to go after it, and you get the nerve to do it.

LORETTA: I think we gave up a little bit too easy at the time we was in Ottawa too. I think we should have kicked up a litle bit more fuss and a little bit more stink, but we was told, "Keep it down here, don't embarrass this one." Well Mr. Baker, he made himself scarce, when 'twas brought up in the House. He didn't show up.

BETTY: They must have been ashamed of us, but we weren't ashamed of ourself. I don't think anybody in politics ever went to bed where they worked that hard in the day that the blood was running out of their fingers. And we done that a good many nights. And I don't think that's anything to be ashamed of.

LORETTA: There was nights when I come in — that was the first year — that I come in and you had to wash, because it's a real dirty job. No *lady* —

BETTY: No, if you was a lady, you wouldn't do it.

LORETTA: But when you sees where there's money and you see where you can better yourself, you're going to do it.

BETTY: It all happens on the spur of the moment.

LORETTA: She pushes. I'm not that big of a fighter but she pushes me. She won't give in. And she got me in trouble like that a lot of times. (Laughter.)

BETTY: I'm stubborn. When I say I'm not going to move, I'm not going to move. Unless somebody moves me. And so far I haven't had a move yet.

LORETTA: I kept me boat rubbers, so long as there's squids. I can't see meself out on the nets. I don't know, but right now I can't see meself — I can go out and jig cod. I like that. I got some up there in the fridge. I don't sell it or anything like that, but I've jigged cod and eat it. But I can't see meself out with lobster pots. You can't get a lobster licence, eh? I think that's something I'd like to do.

There's no squid licence, though. You just go out and do it, the same as you do cod. This is what got us going to squid, eh? 'Twas something we could handle. I mean, 'twas hard work, but we went after it and we got it. The only problem we've had is getting our unemployment.

LORETTA: A friend of mine, she been at squid three years now. Next year, when her husband goes out at the lobster, she's going with him. That's one I knows for sure. And Betty bought her nets, so we intended to go out!

BETTY: I bought the herring nets and never put them in the water. (Laughs.) Two or three years back there was a big quota for herring. It would be on for weeks and everybody could get what they want, right? So I bought the nets. But when I bought the nets they cut the quota! I don't think that had anything to do with me! (Laughs.) But I didn't put any nets out, because it was only a small quota and the men wouldn't appreciate the women at the herring when there's only a small quota.

LORETTA: Well, this year I got a phone call from a packing place to come down and pack squids. This is for labour stamps, this is not fishing stamps.

There's more money in squid, if squid were here, eh? Because they only pay the minimum wage at the packing plant. So where the squid was so scarce, I took the job and went to work. It lasted almost four weeks. I got four stamps down there, and I only got two from squids this year. They were nice-sized stamps.

And packing is a lot easier work. I mean, it's forty-pound boxes I had, packing them and lifting them and weighing them and then bring them back and pack more like that, eh? Lot of lifting. But I found it a lot easier than at the squid.

LORETTA: There's a nice few women really went out after the squid this year. They worked, they had to work. If they had to work any harder than I had to work last year for it, I don't know how they survived, because it took everything I had to do it last year. But a good many changed their minds, eh? There's no way that they could hold up to it. Because it's not only the young people, it's older women, grandmothers.

BETTY: The young people is not that interested.

LORETTA: No, that's right. It's too hard work for them. Couldn't be bothered with all these hours they had to put into it. All the time — no time for housework or anything like that. Which I didn't mind! (Laughs.) Any excuse'll do.

BETTY: Before, on this island, the majority of people only had one income. Now, unemployment insurance is not a big income, but it do keep food on the table all the time for a majority of people. Before they could only have about seventy percent of the groceries they needed because they had all their bills and that to cover. But since they been getting unemployment, the money's been flowing more free. And it's good for the businesses, too.

LORETTA: Now you come in a community like this, or Virgin Arm, and you go on the wharves, and you look and see who's on the wharf most, men or women; you find there's more women.

BETTY: Years ago it was the same thing, the women were at the fish. The men went and caught it, but the women dried it. But they didn't get anything out of it. There was no such thing as unemployment insurance. It's only the past few years that the fishing have picked up around here. But it's ninety percent women and ten percent men.

BETTY: There's some that criticize. Some say the men take their wife off for the weekend, catching trout, and get unemployment stamps for them. And even some women in Ottawa, when we were up there, they actually made fun at us to our face — like, "You didn't do it. It's only propaganda you're going on with," and all this. I'd like to have them for a week.

LORETTA: Our invitation was extended, eh? (Laughs.) Try it, see what you can do of it, eh? You'd see a good many flat on their face.

BETTY: People are beginning to realize that they might as well come across, because women are going to fight to get what they wants. It's been a long time happening, out this way. People will say, "You don't deserve it," and the women will say, "Okay, we don't deserve it, we won't have it then, eh?" But now they're beginning to realize that they *do* deserve it as much as the men, and they're willing to stand up for it. I hope they are.

LORETTA: This is something to look back and tell our grand-children.

BETTY: It might be in the history book. Who knows?

Betty Burt is running a small grocery store out of her home now. Loretta is still squidjigging and last winter collected her unemployment insurance.

— Judy McClard

Jennifer Penney is a health educator at a
Toronto community clinic who has been active
around women's and labour issues for many years.
Besides writing numerous articles, she has
co-authored *Highrise and Superprofits* and is a
contributor to *The Women's Workbook.*

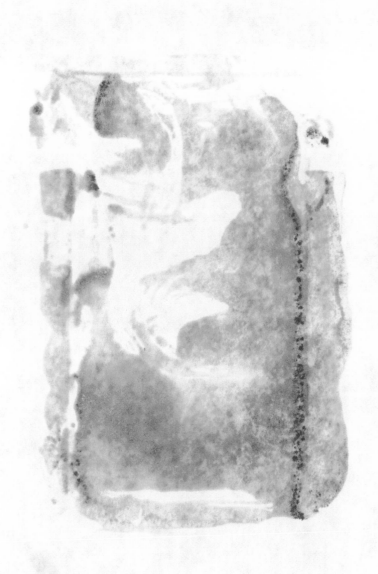

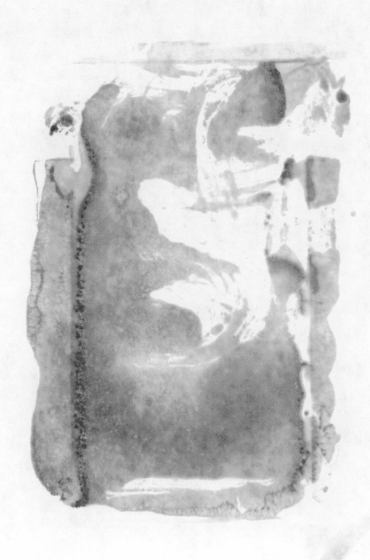